Teaching History

Teaching History

William Caferro

WILEY Blackwell

Registered Office
John Wiley & Sons, Inc., 111 River Street, Hoboken, NJ 07030, USA

Editorial Office
111 River Street, Hoboken, NJ 07030, USA

For details of our global editorial offices, customer services, and more information about Wiley products visit us at www.wiley.com.

Wiley also publishes its books in a variety of electronic formats and by print-on-demand. Some content that appears in standard print versions of this book may not be available in other formats.

Library of Congress Cataloging-in-Publication Data
Names: Caferro, William, author.
Title: Teaching history / Prof William Caferro.
Description: First edition. | Hoboken, NJ : Wiley-Blackwell, 2020. | Includes index. |
Identifiers: LCCN 2019015114 (print) | LCCN 2019015530 (ebook) | ISBN
    9781119147145 (Adobe PDF) | ISBN 9781119147152 (ePub) | ISBN 9781119147121
    (hardcover) | ISBN 9781119147138 (pbk.)
Subjects: LCSH: History–Study and teaching (Secondary).
Classification: LCC D16.2 (ebook) | LCC D16.2 .C24 2020 (print) | DDC 907.1/2–dc23
LC record available at https://lccn.loc.gov/2019015114

Cover Design: Wiley
Cover Image: © kyoshino/Getty Images

Set in 10/12pt Warnock by SPi Global, Pondicherry, India
Printed and bound in Singapore by Markono Print Media Pte Ltd

10 9 8 7 6 5 4 3 2 1

Contents

Contents

Acknowledgments

This book is dedicated to my teachers, colleagues and students, who have meant more to me than I can express here. The classroom has been my "safe space" throughout my career, the site where I do what has always meant the most to me, teaching. I wish first to thank the principal of my high school (James Madison High), Ira Ewen, who impressed upon us that learning is a life-long process that teaching is intended to spark. I thank also Al Williams, dean of Haverford College, who convinced me to return to college despite the culture shock and my teenage stupidity. I was fortunate to have wonderful professors at Bryn Mawr, where I majored in History, and Yale University, where I studied the Middle Ages. It has been my unique privilege to have worked with John Boswell, Jim Boyden, Charles Brand, Jane Caplan, Arthur Dudden, Jaroslav Pelikan, Bentley Layton, Harry Miskimin and Frank M. Turner. I would not have found a college job after the premature death of my advisors without the "beyond the call of duty" efforts of Jim Boyden, Harry Miskimin and Frank Turner.

A basic lesson learned from writing this volume is that professors have very strong feelings about teaching methods, more forceful in some cases than those they have about their academic work. The fact that the former is rarely discussed openly may account for the intensity of views. I wish to thank Tess Harvey, who first contacted me with the idea for this book in 2014, and Peter Coveney for encouraging me to pursue the project despite sometimes withering critique. I am grateful to Janani Govindankutty and Niranjana Vallavan for their practical help, good will and advice with the manuscript and images, and Jennifer Manias for the same, and for bringing the endeavor to life.

The book is the product of a long and varied (uneven) career in the classroom, beginning with a broken blackboard as a high school math teacher in Queens New York in 1985, followed by many subsequent twists, turns and incarnations. I thank the many scholar/teachers who have discussed teaching with me in many different settings, including my colleagues in secondary school: Larry Belascu, Tom Butler, Ed Dempsey,

Dick Dolven, Bill Hunter, Cindy Jones, Stacey Lorenz, Fred Richter, Whit Russell, Bob Schroeder, Fred Wesson and Shelley Rigger; and my colleagues in college: William Abbott, Patricia Behre, Richard Blackett, Brad Bradley, Jonathan Bremer, Brandi Brimmer, Cecelia Bucki, Tom Buckley, Tom Buoye, David Carlton, Lauren Clay, Simon Collier, Ralph Coury, Dennis Dickerson, Don Doyle, Robert Drews, Devin Fergus, Kim Hanger, Joel Harrington, Walter Petry, Rick DeAngelis, Eldon Eisenach, Jim Epstein, Kathy Gaca, Leor Halevi, Leon Helguerra, Jeff Hockett, Jacob Howland, Russell Hittinger, August Johnson, Sarah Igo, Peter Lake, Jane Landers, Phil Lieberman, Paul Lim, Peter Lorge, Leah Marcus, Tom Martin, Laura McDaniel, Tom McGinn, Sam McSeveney, David McFadden, Rowena Olegario, John Plummer, Paul Rahe, Matt Ramsey, Joe Rife, Ruth Rogaski, Tom Schwartz, Dan Solomon, Helmut Smith, Mary Lee Townsend, Arleen Tuchman and David Wasserstein. There are many others, and I apologize to those I have left out.

I wish to express especial gratitude to Caroline Walker Bynum, who read drafts of the early chapters, generously took the time from an incredibly busy schedule to talk with me at length about the project and connect me with colleagues across the profession. There has been no better teacher and mentor in my field. I single out also my distinguished Vanderbilt colleagues Michael Bess and Marshall Eakin, who are the guiding spirit behind the Vanderbilt graduate teaching seminar; Frank Wcislo, with whom I have had animated talks about teaching for nearly two decades; Christopher Loss, who helped in every way with the project and gave detailed and wonderful suggestions for reading, and Joe Bandy and Derek Bruff of the Teaching Center at Vanderbilt, who respectively read drafts and discussed teaching strategies with me.

Finally, I thank those professors who took time – often considerable amounts of it – to discuss their teaching strategies and experiences with me: Michael Bess, Ari Bryen, Marshall Eakin, Catherine Molineux, John Plummer, Ole Molvig and Moses Ochonu of Vanderbilt University; Sam Cohn of the University of Glasgow; Jennifer Spock of Eastern Kentucky University; Devin Fergus of the University of Missouri; Laura Hohman of Trivecca Nazarene College; Anthony Molho of Brown and the European University; Richard Davis of Bard College; Corey Tazzara of Scripps College; Hilmar Pabel of Simon Fraser University; Paul Rahe of Hillsdale College; Samantha Kelly of Rutgers University; Hoyt Tillman of Arizona State University; Wendy Doninger of the University of Chicago; Steven Epstein of University of Kansas; Susan Mosher Stuard of Haverford College; Neslihan Senocak and Joel Kaye of Columbia University; Kay Reyerson of the University of Minnesota; and Daniel Genkins and Aileen Teague, post-docs at Brown University, and J'Nese Williams, a post-doc at Stanford, who were also members in the graduate teaching seminar I taught.

Introduction

My old friends smile at me when I talk about teaching. They know me as a profoundly introverted person, who spoke little in school and even less outside of it. Nevertheless, it was in the context of school – public school in NYC, private colleges in Pennsylvania and New Haven – that I became intellectually engaged and personally transformed. My intention early on was to teach, if for no other reason than to find another introverted person, too nervous to raise his/her hand in class, lacking ambition and let them know that there is a world of possibilities out there and that those possibilities begin with education.

After 35 years of teaching, starting in high school and now in college, the profession seems more complex than ever. The advent of online and digital technologies has changed the nature of the classroom, while academe itself continues to morph and redefine itself. David Staley and Dennis Trinkle in an important essay speak of "seismic changes" in the landscape of higher education.[1] Robert Bellah tells of stratification, of "winners and losers" in the academic game: the former holding full-time tenured positions, the latter representing a growing underclass of overworked part-time and adjunct faculty, whose labor is cheap.[2] School administration has become progressively staffed by professionals, often with different world views from faculty, while a new species of "culture wars" engulf campuses. Debates over effective pedagogy have correspondingly intensified and are at least as contentious as those in academic disciplines.

This is not surprising. Teaching is, like the scholarly writing it is often opposed to, intrinsically bound up with who we are, how we perceive ourselves, and how we wish others to perceive us. College professors may argue that the one activity takes away from the other, but the two rest on

1 David J. Staley and Dennis A. Trinkle, The changing landscape of higher education. *Educause Review* (2011), p. 16.
2 Robert Bellah, Class wars and culture wars. *Academe* July/August (1997), p. 23.

Teaching History, First Edition. William Caferro.

strikingly similar foundations. Both are visceral in nature, and we invest a great deal of ourselves in them. We imagine that we should at once master them, and feel a special sense of disappointment when we do not.

The last point alone makes the present inquiry worthwhile, along with the unsettling fact that fiscal and professional rewards for teaching are far less than those for writing. Good teaching often goes unrewarded. My graduate professor, Harry Miskimin, put the issue bluntly: "You know what we do with good teachers at Yale? We fire them!" He was being ironic, but the point was served. Yale professors wrote books and articles; teaching belonged to its own separate subcategory.

"Professor Smith learns how not to get tenure."

Source: AcademicKeys.com

The opposition of research and teaching is, however, not only unhelpful, but it has the effect of sharpening divides in the already fragmented academic landscape. It encourages a similarly righteous tone among those dedicated to the "lesser" art. Teaching is difficult, time-consuming and, most importantly, highly rewarding work. And it is, in the strictest sense of the word, an art. The path to success is, however, not immediately clear. In his excellent *Aims of Teaching*, Kenneth Eble spoke in biblical terms of the "seven deadly" sins that impede good teaching. His list includes, among others, "dullness, self-indulgence and arrogance" – traits that none of us want to be associated with.[3] Stephen Brookfield states bluntly that

---

3 Eble's full list includes arrogance, dullness, rigidity, insensitivity, vanity, self-indulgence, hypocrisy, sloth, and pride. Kenneth Eble, *The Aims of College Teaching* (San Francisco: Jossey-Bass, 1983), p. 93. See also Grant P. Wiggins and Jay McTighe, *Understanding by Design* (Alexandria: Association for Supervision and Curriculum Development, 1998).

teachers must learn the difficult lesson "that the sincerity of their intentions does not guarantee the purity of their practice."[4] Barbara Harrell Carson's interviews with former students at Rollins College show that they remember bad classroom experiences and "bad professors" more than 30 years later![5]

The evidence makes clearer still the importance of teaching The present question is how to achieve success in the classroom? For the PhD candidates in our "Art and Craft of Teaching History" at Vanderbilt, the answer is, unfortunately, "quickly." They are placed in front of classes before they are ready, first as TAs and then, if lucky, as overburdened and undercompensated assistant professors. Some embrace the challenge, some do not. They nevertheless must sustain themselves at a time when they are most vulnerable, face obstacles both pedagogical and personal, not the least of which includes dealing with students so close to them in age that their authority is not always easily accepted.

Unfortunately, the impediments outlined above do not necessarily disappear with time. They more precisely morph and continue to confront teachers in one way or another throughout their careers. They are not equally shared, and involve also issues of race, gender, ethnicity, and class (among still others) that will be discussed at greater length in the final chapter. The aim of this volume is to show how professors have approached these challenges and the many ways in which they have achieved success and contentment. The discussion is inclusive, drawing on pedagogical literature and conversations with colleagues, young and old, across the history profession, who have shared their experiences and opinions. I make no claim for profession expertise; I am, like the many colleagues I have spoken with over the years, "a lifer," not a spokesperson. I have taught in both secondary school and college. The main focus of the book is primarily on teaching the history of the distant, non-American past, which I know best and am most familiar with. The academy has broadened the range of courses it teaches in recent years to include much more of the non-Anglophone world, but it remains the case that nearly all of the excellent books about university teaching focus on American history and extrapolate advice from that field. For the sake of honesty, my approach must necessarily diverge. Nevertheless, the notions of historical and critical thinking advocated by pedagogical experts like Sam Wineberg, Bruce VanSledright, L. Dee Fink, Stephen Brookfield, Grant Wiggins, and Jay McTighe and on web pages like those of the National

4 Stephen Brookfield, *Becoming a Critically Reflective Teacher* (San Francisco: Jossey-Bass, 1995). p. 28.
5 Barbara Harrell Carson, Bad news in the service of good teaching. *Journal on Excellence in College Teaching*, 10:1, pp. 91–92.

Council for History Education (NCHE), the Stanford History Group and others are applicable and indeed vital to learning in all historical fields.

I underline the term <u>inclusive</u>. While this book seeks to affirm the rewards of teaching and the various roads to success, it rejects out of hand writings that rail against straw man pedagogy. I for one have never met Lendol Calder's "tweedy professor" with his "pull-down maps and chalkboards" and complete unawareness of his craft and understanding of his students.[6] I think I saw him in the film *The Paper Chase*, but not in my real-life experience. Similarly, I have encountered few colleagues who, as Joel Sipress and David Voelker maintain in a recent essay, are slavishly devoted to a "coverage model" in their introductory classes.[7] I saw this in high school, but the professors I know assign books and readings that they like, that often have personal meaning to them, and meet practical criteria, like being readily available on the internet or at a fair price (a big challenge) at the bookstore. Nevertheless, I completely agree with Calder's call for a "signature pedagogy" and Sipress and Voelker's adherence to "working backward" in designing courses, focusing on a few desired learning outcomes and a few key ideas.

It is an undeniable fact that in our lifetimes, we take classes from many different teachers, who impress us in many different ways. My high school math teacher, Mrs Simon, seemed oblivious to whatever pedagogy ruled in those days. She projected a sincerity and enthusiasm that seemed to simplify the task at hand. She made you feel like you too could do the hardest problem, because she could. She made no effort to impress. Her explanations were simple, straightforward, and effective. She "flipped" the classroom long before that word became part of the pedagogical lexicon, having us do the work together on the board. I got my start standing up in front of class in that context, and found an intellectual self-confidence even while adolescence denied me any of the personal variety. I went to college as a math major because of her.

My college history professor, Charles Brand, by contrast, was intellectually forbidding and severe. It followed well his field, Byzantium, which is obscure even to those of us who study the Middle Ages. He typed his notes, seldom looked beyond them and had a pronounced stutter (I can still hear him trying to say "Heraclius," the name of an early Byzantine emperor). Yet, his deep-rooted engagement in the material was utterly endearing, genuine and rubbed off on all of us. I became a history major. My graduate advisor John Boswell wore a Mickey Mouse watch, a

---

6 Lendol Calder, Uncoverage: toward a signature pedagogy for the history survey. *Journal of American History*, 92 (2006), pp. 1358–1359.

7 Joel Sipress and David Voelker, The end of the history survey course: the rise and fall of the coverage model. *Journal of American History*, 97 (2011), pp. 1050–1066.

baseball cap on his head, and looked about 10 years younger than the students he taught. But he stood sovereign before the class, employing well-timed jokes to make very serious points. The practice made his unique mastery of his subject all the more apparent. He cited works in Arabic, Latin, and Greek. Above all, he exuded pure joy, a sense of play, as he taught. He lectured on medieval sexuality long before the subject became part of university curricula, founded the then Lesbian and Gay Studies Center at Yale University and was open about his own sexuality as a gay man. He was, I thought then, a latter-day Anselm of Canterbury, a living example of "faith seeking understanding," comfortable with himself and compassionate of others. The message was powerful and clear. It is OK to be yourself, whoever you are, and it is cool to be completely engaged in what you do. I keep a photo of John in the top drawer of my office desk at school. If he had the courage to be himself in the academy, then maybe I could too. I would not be a professional medievalist if I had not met him.

The point here is that it is important that we not define too narrowly the road to success and the elements of good teaching. Each of the above-mentioned people was comfortable with themselves, organized and deeply engaged in the material they taught. They possessed an authenticity, a talent and enthusiasm for explaining, and an empathy for the students in their charge – qualities that Ken Bain has highlighted in his well-known study of excellent teachers.[8] We project our lives onto theirs, extrapolate, imagine ourselves as similarly engaged, skilled and prepossessed – in whatever we ultimately choose to do.

It is somewhere in all this that I locate myself, an inadequate and contingent being, who is nevertheless deeply engaged in learning, who through love of that – and very careful preparation and organization – is able to get outside of himself (at least a few days a week) and express that to others.

This is, however, not unique to any individual. The varied and voluminous literature on college teaching – an academic subfield of its own – allows us to generalize the following: effective teachers are those who convey their love of learning, know their material well, show concern for the students they teach and get their students to engage in active learning. And what is important about the Scholarship of Teaching and Learning (SoTL) and other current trends in the art of pedagogy is that, like all good programs, they encourage us to look more closely at what we do, to be more aware of how students respond to us and to seek "student-centered" strategies to bring our scholarly selves more in line with our

---

8 Ken Bain, *What the Best College Teachers Do* (Cambridge: Harvard University Press, 2004), pp. 15–16.

teacherly selves. The work of cognitive scientists and conversations across disciplines have allowed teachers to better understand how students learn and be better able to relativize their own teaching styles in terms of others.[9]

I echo Ken Bain's hope that "readers will take away from this book the conviction that good teaching can be learned."[10] I also echo Bain's concern that teaching is an endeavor "that seldom learns from its past" because the "insights" of professors often "die with them." But teachers have to "find their own genius" and adjust their methods to who they are and what they teach.[11] Whether one stands as an advocate of a new method or as "tweedy" champion of the *ancien régime*, teachers must remember not only how to talk with each other, but how to continue to talk with students, even as their worlds appear to recede further from each other.

***

The volume is divided into five chapters, each of which deals with an aspect of teaching history. The first chapter discusses the strategies employed by professors to initially prepare for class. It evaluates the challenges they face, the philosophy embedded in their methods and efforts to engage students in active learning and historical thinking. The second chapter examines teaching history in historical perspective. It traces the development of the discipline from the early days through the "big bang" in US higher education (1870–1915) to the modern day. It takes the long view of the profession in order to contextualize it and better assess teaching methods, which, owing to a dearth of such studies, are too often assumed rather than carefully assayed. Indeed, the divides that separate professors are to a degree based on the erection of straw men on each side. The chapter also examines the status of the field in a continually changing political and educational landscape. The tradition of the profession affects the way we teach.[12]

---

9 Peter Felton, Principles of good practice in SoTL. *Teaching & Learning Inquiry*, 1:1 (2013), p. 123; on critical thinking, see Stéphane Lévesque, *Thinking Historically: Educating Students for the Twenty- First Century* (Toronto: University of Toronto Press, 2008); Peter Stearns, Peter Seixas and Sam Wineburg, eds. *Knowing, Teaching, & Learning History. National and International Perspectives* (New York: New York University Press, 2000); Laurie Richlin, *Blueprint for Learning: Constructing College Courses to Facilitate, Assess, and Document Learning* (Sterling: Stylus Publishing, 2006).
10 Ken Bain, *What the Best College Teachers Do*, p. 21.
11 Ken Bain, *What the Best College Teachers Do*, pp. 3, 21.
12 Louis Menand, *The Marketplace of Ideas: Reform and Resistance in the American University* (New York: Norton, 2010), p. 97.

Chapter 3 looks at practical issues involving course management. It examines ineffective classroom experiences and what professors do to overcome and avoid them. It discusses issues of class management, assignments (reading, writing, and research papers) and techniques used to elicit discussion, present lectures, and grade student work. Chapter 4 deals explicitly with technology, the rapid growth of which has opened up new possibilities in classroom teaching, while sharpening generational divides. It explores opinions about the "dos" and "don'ts" of deploying technology, the utility of MOOCs and online classes, the hazards of PowerPoint and the outlook for the future. The final chapter examines historians and their professional milieu. It assesses how professors navigate institutional, departmental, and professional politics and broader sociological and cultural issues at play in the academy.

The idea for this book derives in the first instance from my experience as instructor of "The Art and Craft of Teaching" at Vanderbilt University for our second-year graduate students. It is a semester-long seminar intended to prepare students for teaching and more generally to face "what comes next." I was invited to teach it by my talented and committed colleagues Marshall Eakin and Michael Bess, who are responsible for the content and ethos of the class. My involvement was reluctant and I confess that when the course was first proposed, I was against its adoption. I disliked it because I had been a secondary school teacher, trained in the emerging "student-centered" approaches to learning and was skeptical of the ability of college professors – myself above all – to teach pedagogy in that context. Professors are often not trained in this, and I frankly feared the impulse to try to recreate myself in our students. My wife had taken a course on teaching in graduate school in which fellow students presented hypothetical undergraduate lectures to each other. She felt intimidated by the "performative" aspects of teaching she witnessed, believing, like so many people, that good teachers are "born" not made – and that it helped to be extroverted.

I was at the time struggling with the daily routine of preparing high school classes – six a day to be precise – facing the realities of classroom management and hoping simply to survive. Any idealized notions of pedagogy went out the window as I tried to create order from chaos – which was far more difficult than I had imagined. I became aware that presenting myself as anything other than myself – whatever that was – would not work in front of the highly intuitive and hyperperceptive students. And I learned that getting the students to think critically and move beyond intellectual passivity and the tendency, as Bruce VanSledright argues, to view history as "decontextualized, disembodied, authorless forms of neutral information" was a challenging goal.

This book is thus also the product of those secondary school experiences and many others over the years. The classroom has been, to coopt a phrase, "a safe space" for me, where the return has been proportional to the investment. And it should be said that for all the efforts of scholars like Wineberg and VanSledright to bridge the gap between secondary school and college teaching, the reality on the ground for those of us who have worked in both venues is that they remain all too separate and, indeed, often suspicious of one another. The initial review of this manuscript reminded me of this when a critic decried my inclusion of a section on "classroom management" because it is "more appropriate for a book about teaching secondary school than on the college level." Classroom management is important at any level. And for those who staunchly oppose "teacher-centered" education in contrast to "student-centered" education, it is vital that they not extend this distinction, as too often occurs, to a facile opposition of "learning facts" and "learning how to think." As Stéphane Lévesque notes in his *Thinking Historically: Educating Students for the Twenty-First Century*, "too often the current discussion among educators has taken the simple form of supposing an unbridgeable gap between content versus skills."[13] It is in fact possible to do both.

My hope is that the foregoing discussion will make clear that teaching can be taught and that there are indeed many paths to success. Patricia Nelson Limerick, director of the Teaching Center at the University of Colorado, strikes the right note when she observes that academia often attracts people interested in the first instance in a contemplative life "of sustained, lonely labor," but who, by means of "the awful trick of the profession," are cast out of their intellectual refuge and sent into a classroom, where they suddenly become the center of all things.[14] She compares the experience to Christians being fed to lions.

The experiences are not all the same; reaction to us, as will be noted throughout, differs according to race, gender, age, appearance, and a variety of other factors. My experiences as secondary school teacher, which was my first career choice, are so vivid that I can still recite the names of all the students in my first-year classes (in Queens). I returned home after college to teach in the inner city from where I had come on account of the class consciousness of a young person who had grown up with a single parent, who had gone no further than eighth grade. I wanted to put my private college training and personal good fortune to use for

---

13 Stéphane Lévesque, *Thinking Historically: Educating Students for the Twenty-First Century*, p. 20.
14 Patricia Nelson Limerick, Aloof professors and shy students. In: *On Teaching*, edited by Mary Ann Shea, vol. 1 (Boulder: University of Colorado, 1987), p. 2.

others. My college degree in fact almost did not happen because when confronted with the unfamiliar environment of a small, private liberal college, I decided after two years to quit college, which I believed I was unsuited for and which, as I told the dean in an exit interview, was in my opinion then, "a bourgeois plot," intended to reinforce the ascendency of privileged classes. The dean, Al Williams, a professor of color in an almost exclusively white school, smiled at me as he listened, complimented my rhetoric and called me "a sterling idiot," who would hopefully one day – and soon – understand that colleges and new environments represented opportunities.

I left anyway, and took a job programing a mainframe computer at World Trade Center II, as we called it then, for the New York State Department of Epidemiology. I stayed up nights reading history and during that time mentally shifted from math major to historian, personalizing my education, while also learning that being a "regular guy," as I had said to the dean I wanted to be, was not what I supposed. It is a measure of the twists and turns of academic life that Al Williams' daughter, Julia, would later be my advisee at Vanderbilt University.

Teaching high school was the most rewarding and difficult job I ever had. I worked first as a math teacher and then, shifting schools to be closer to my girlfriend (now my wife), as a history teacher (and math teacher in summer school). I ultimately left because I selfishly wanted to focus more on my own studies, learn languages, write books, and feared that the administrative jobs offered me as a reward at a young age would overwhelm my life and eliminate the time to do the things that had brought me to the classroom in the first place. I have never felt entirely comfortable with my decision. Then as now, I believed that we have a greater impact on younger students. For that reason, I make no judgments about the career choices that my students take. As long as they are engaged, self-reflective, doing something meaningful for themselves that makes them happy (and does not harm anyone), then their choice is for the greater good. And I have found in the university setting greater synergies between research and teaching, though this need not necessarily be the case. And having started in math, where economy of expression and working actively together on problems are critical, I had a useful paradigm for history instruction, which requires much the same.

As Dana Goldstein says in her brilliant *The Teacher Wars*, secondary (and primary) school teaching is the "most controversial profession in America."[15] One necessarily grows up in that venue. When I went to graduate school, it was with a sense of purpose that had eluded me to that

---

15 Dana Goldstein, *The Teacher Wars: A History of America's Most Embattled Profession* (New York: Anchor Books, 2014), p. 1.

point in my life and which, I believe, is how all students should approach professional school. I was not interested in the PhD, but wanted to add researching and writing to my life, which is a privilege and a pleasure, and return to the classroom. The process itself is, and should be, as much fun as the result.

After graduate school I moved straight into unemployment. I tried to ignore, as much as possible, the existential and professional obstacles before me. My first university job was as an adjunct at Fairfield University, a Jesuit college in Connecticut, followed by a tenure track position at the University of Tulsa, a small private school in Oklahoma. The job was eliminated after my third year and I was fortunate to land at Vanderbilt University, where I have taught medieval European and economic history for the past 20 years. The trajectory has given me a deep appreciation for experiences of teachers at various levels and stages, as well as an understanding of the Calvinist nature of the academic universe, where people of the same skills, talents, and work ethic often land in very different places.

It may sound like a contradiction in this venue, but I wish to add that I do not perceive of the classes that I teach as of singular importance. I see them in a broader perspective as part of an array of university courses that students take – myself as one of the many teachers they come into contact with. I subscribe to the view, first articulated to me and my friends in high school by our principal Mr Ewen, that we become truly educated only when we realize that we alone are responsible for our education. He would tell us that a person could get a better education by going to the New York Public Library every day than by going to New York Public School. It was only the latter, however, that bestowed a degree. In this spirit, college courses should provide a spark, an entrée into the larger intellectual world and the tools for independent learning. If students leave our classes never wanting to learn more about history then we will have failed as historians, whatever our approach. Measurable learning goals, as Raymond J. Shaw argues, march along with immeasurable ones, including life revelations, transformations that may not manifest themselves until after the fact.[16] Historians are in the business of lifelong learning.

---

16 Raymond J. Shaw, Assessing the intangible in our students (2017). www.chronicle.com/article/assessing-the-intangible-in/240744

1

The Art and Craft of Teaching, or Toward a Philosophy of Teaching

Source: CartoonStock.com

> Other people can talk about how to expand the destiny of mankind. I just want to talk about how to fix a motorcycle. I think that what I have to say has more lasting value. (Robert M. Pirsig, *Zen and the Art of Motorcycle Maintenance: An Inquiry Into Values*[1])

Pirsig's famous statement favors praxis over theory. It is of course a theory of its own, and a profound one. It applies well to classroom teaching, especially at the beginning of one's career.

---

1 Robert M. Pirsig, *Zen and the Art of Motorcycle Maintenance: An Inquiry into Values* (New York: Bantom, 1988), p. 267.

Teaching History, First Edition. William Caferro.
© 2020 John Wiley & Sons, Inc. Published 2020 by John Wiley & Sons, Inc.

We want to fix the motorcycle! We stand before the masses (our students) not in search of a philosophy in the first instance, but in search of a practical way forward. There is little time to contemplate the destiny of mankind or the meaning of the universe. Teaching is instinctive, human, and, I would submit, its own obstacle to theoretical inquiry insofar as once the skill is learned, it seems more of a technical or interpersonal one than an intellectual one. Teaching is, as Parker Palmer famously asserted, a triumph of the will and soul.[2] But it is *our* motorcycle. We fix it (teach) behind closed doors. In this way, teaching is also, as Palmer asserts, "the most privatized of public professions."[3] Many instructors spend their lives "bound in chains of silence."[4]

There are nevertheless transcendent issues at play, no matter how much we may wish to ignore them. Indeed, few endeavors have engendered more ardent philosophical discussions than teaching. Allan Bloom in *Closing of the American Mind* believed that the fate of western democracy lay in balance in American classrooms. He spoke, as his title suggests, pessimistically, blaming the abandonment of the study of western classics on "cultural relativists" and "fans of rock music" whom he cast as enemies of the state.[5] Gary Nash and his colleagues struggled in their attempt to establish national standards for the study of American history in the 1990s owing to the deeply political nature of the subject matter.[6]

The confluence of these factors perhaps explains why the literature on university teaching often begins with discussions of "anxiety." Elaine Showalter describes anxiety in her *Teaching Literature* as the inevitable handmaiden of teaching, even for the most experienced veterans. She tells of vivid dreams before the first day of classes, including one in which she inexplicably skipped class for weeks, only to arrive breathless and illegally parked.[7] Jane Thompson expressed her fears in a series of fictive postcards to herself and to colleagues that expose self-doubt and personal insecurity.[8] Douglas A. Bernstein admits that the "severe" suffering he experienced at the beginning of his career has never left him.[9]

---

2 Parker Palmer, *The Courage to Teach* (San Francisco: Jossy-Bass, 2007, 10th edition), pp. 1–3.
3 Parker Palmer, *The Courage to Teach*, p. 2.
4 Stephen D. Brookfield, *Becoming a Critically Reflective* Teacher (San Francisco: Jossey-Bass, 1995), p. 247.
5 Allan Bloom, *The Closing of the American Mind* (New York: Simon & Schuster, 1987).
6 Gary B. Nash, Charlotte Crabtree and Ross E. Dunn, *History of Trial: Culture Wars and the Teaching of the Past* (New York: Vintage Books, first published 1994).
7 Elaine Showalter, *Teaching Literature* (Malden: Blackwell, 2003), p. 5.
8 Jane Thompson, *What a Teacher Learned* (Reading,: Perseus Books, 1996).
9 Douglas A. Bernstein, Dealing with teaching anxiety. *NACTA Journal* December (1983), p. 4.

It is easy to relate. We all worry about how we are perceived by others and, more generally, how to deal with the "performative" aspects of the profession. For me, it is not about tortured dreams but lack of them. I do not sleep well before the first day of class. This has been true for 30 years. A high school teacher colleague of mine told me it was a good sign. It showed that I cared. "May you never sleep well before teaching!" At this point in my life I would rather sleep, since there are few things I enjoy more. And many of my colleagues, who care at least as much as I do about teaching, sleep very well before the start of class. They are both effective and *well rested* on the first day!

The point is, however, that there are many paths to success – a theme that will be stressed throughout this book. It is, as Patricia Nelson Limerick says, "our First Amendment right" to be nervous. And telling professors to relax "just makes us more weird."[10] And with all due respect to the very fine professors who highlight their anxieties, I for one believe that too much has been written about the subject. The discussions border on self-indulgence. It is true that we worry, but so too do workers in hospitals, fire stations, legal offices, and many other jobs. Moreover, contemplation of worry does not necessarily help the beginning teacher move forward in the classroom. "Sure I am anxious, but how do I practically succeed?" Anxiety is for them a bourgeois emotion. To the extent that acknowledging our fears helps us manage them, the discussions are useful. But the working person needs more.

The challenge for the teacher in the first instance is to find a means of communicating with the students, who are dealing with their own set of anxieties. We do well to contemplate the worries of students, however arcane and strange their worlds may on the surface seem to us. The approach turns the psychology around. It encourages us to imagine the class from their perspective, which is a relief from our own anxieties.

The notion was made plain to me on my very first day as a teacher in high school. An older colleague watched me (age 22) fidgeting in the faculty room, completely focused on myself, hoping to do well in my first appearance "on stage." She came over and said "You are aware it is *their* first day, right Caferro?" I had not given "them" any thought at all, except in terms of how they would view me. The advice really helped. It was in fact the best advice I have ever had. She turned the psychology to where it belonged.

The message is now a mantra. The best way to get the most out of the students is to construct an environment and structures in which they can

---

10 Patricia Nelson Limerick, Aloof professors and shy students. In: *On Teaching*, edited by Mary Ann Shea, vol. 1 (Boulder: University of Colorado, 1987), p. 3.

succeed, in which they want to succeed, and, more generally, are able see clearly the requirements for success. The approach does not assure that you will be perceived as a "great" teacher but it is a first step toward basic competence. It provides an "out" from long self-involved contemplations of one's teaching persona. It allows us to get beyond the cult of personality, which is more suited to some people than to others. And it is an important first step toward establishing "student-centered," active learning.[11]

We do indeed bare our souls in front of the class, but it is more effective if we do not do so consciously. The students see our personalities whether we want them to or not. Given that, it seems more efficacious to focus on the motorcycle, as it were – on practical issues such as presentation of the course material and organization of the class engagement of students in critical thought (see Chapter 3). These reveal our relationship with our subject matter and with the immediate task before us. This is teachable. The image of an engaged, organized teacher is a compelling one, and can be as different from one person to another as our personalities. If our personalities inevitably and subconsciously come through, so too does our attitude toward our subject matter. As a student, I admired all my teachers who loved learning, cared deeply about their subject matter and had a clear organizational structure that they adhered to, provoked new ideas and questions, and had basic empathy, expressed in their own unique ways.

A Teaching Philosophy

With all this in mind, the first assignment we give our graduate students in our seminar on pedagogy at Vanderbilt ("Art and Craft of Teaching History") is to write a philosophy of teaching. The assignment is unpopular. The graduates see it as putting the cart before the horse or, worse, the sort of "touchy feely" task that augurs a long boring semester. But fixing a motorcycle is, as Pirsig makes clear, its own philosophy. We sell the assignment to the students by stressing its practicality. It will be useful when they apply for jobs and later when they go up for promotion. Indeed, one of the positive recent developments in the academy is that job committees often ask candidates to send teaching statements, along with syllabi of prospective courses, for their "job talk." The job talk used to consist primarily of a lecture on research. It is now divided into a

---

11 Stéphane Lévesque, *Thinking Historically: Educating Students for the Twenty-First Century* (Toronto: University of Toronto Press, 2008), pp. 17–19.

research-related lecture and a demonstration of teaching, the latter sometimes an informal discussion of teaching in seminar fashion, which amounts to a discussion of teaching philosophy. The teaching demonstration is in many ways more difficult for the candidate than the research lecture. Aspiring professors come into direct contact for the first time with competing ideologies and methodologies. The host history faculty may know nothing of the candidates' research subfield, but they usually have opinions – and strong ones – about teaching.

In addition to its professional practicality, the exercise is also useful because it encourages self-reflection. The graduates are forced to think more directly about their objectives and, in some cases, confront the reality that they will indeed stand before a class. The American historian Peter Filene recommends this sort of reflection for all starting professors. He suggests that we answer five fill-in-the-blank questions ("prompts"), including "In class I see myself as (blank)" and "I seek to foster in my students (blank)."[12]

To aid the students in our seminar, we give them the teaching statements of their own professors in the History department – those who graciously allow them to be read. There is, to be sure, irony. The statement of teaching philosophy was in my generation something we did only when we came up for promotion, seven years into our careers (if lucky). My high school colleagues scoff at the very idea of a teaching philosophy written by a college professor. Secondary school teachers have often read extensively the literature on pedagogy. They have discussed it with colleagues and committees specifically tasked with evaluating their performance, and applied it in real time and space before students. We often fly by the seat of our pants, waxing philosophical only when we need to impress a tenure committee. And as terrible as it is to admit, my colleagues and I in fact exchanged our statements with each other, essentially passing them down to the next person in the tenure line, nuancing the statements along the way. I used Helmut Smith's statement, who followed Michael Bess, who presumably followed someone else. The aim was more to pass muster with the administration than to gain any real insight into teaching. At least it was for me.

But as a teaching tool, discussion of the statements of endeavor is useful. It becomes obvious when reading them that they do indeed reveal the souls of their authors. They project stored up experiences and strategies employed and, most immediately, they form the basis of a discussion on teaching – the very thing that Parker Palmer, Ken Bain, and others have

---

12 Peter Filene, *The Joy of Teaching: A Practical Guide for New College Instructors* (Chapel Hill: University of North Carolina Press, 2005), pp. 11–12.

pointed out as most lacking in the profession. Michael Bess, who teaches a popular course at Vanderbilt on World War II, stresses the importance of raising "moral" issues with students. He sees his role as getting students to question their beliefs. Marshall Eakin, a professor of modern Latin American history, stresses the importance of the "big picture" in history. He believes in a classroom structure that emphasizes writing and attendance. He expresses the hope that his students will use their education to become more involved in the public sphere.

The statements elicit a strong response from the students. Much of it, perhaps surprisingly, is disagreement. Should a teacher involve herself/ himself in moral or political issues in class? Is my own subject matter suitable for involvement in the public sphere? Will I be a stern professor or a more accommodating one? Will any of this stuff work for someone my age, race, ethnicity, and background (see Chapter 5)?

Some graduate students already have a strong sense of what they will do. They are in tune with a Hegelian world spirit that makes them sure they will be successful. Others have no idea what they will do. The teaching statements initiate a conversation that rarely takes place verbally, indeed rarely takes place at all among colleagues or with professors and their students.

The Good Teacher

Philosophy is, however, no substitute for experience. In the best parts of her discussion of anxiety, Elaine Showalter highlights lack of adequate training for young teachers. Peter Filene in his *The Joy of Teaching* asserts that it takes "three run-throughs" for even an experienced professor to fashion a course to their liking.[13] Robert Boice's study of first-year university faculty shows that they equated good teaching with "good content."[14] The Harriet W. Sheridan Center for Teaching at Brown University suggests that new professors allow themselves enough time to go through several iterations of their syllabi.[15] Here, the difference between college and secondary school is great. In my home state of Tennessee, initiatives such as the Memphis Teacher Residency advocate "hands-on" experience

---

13 Peter Filene, *The Joy of Teaching*, p. 1.
14 Robert Boice, Quick starters: new faculty who succeed. In: *Effective Practices for Improving Teaching: New Directions for Teaching and Learning*, edited by Michael Theall and Jennifer Franklin (San Francisco: Jossey-Bass, 1991), pp. 111–112.
15 Harriet W. Sheridan Center for Teaching at Brown University. www.brown.edu/ sheridan/programs-services

for novice secondary school teachers and mentor them via direct experience in the classroom for a full year with a full-time teacher.[16]

This does little to help the beginning professor. And it is unhelpful, nay disingenuous, to tell beginners, as I was told as a young PhD, to cut corners when faced with limited time. It is difficult to cut corners when you do not have mastery of the subject material or full understanding of the medium. The better advice, however unwanted, is to work hard, but wisely, when preparing (see Chapter 3).

I posed the question to colleagues, asking what practical basic steps they used to get ready for class. "I try to keep it simple," the medievalist Steven Epstein at the University of Kansas says. "I lay out a distinct trajectory for the course on the first day, with clearly stated themes, usually only a few. We then work off these and I try to be open to whatever deviation occurs in class discussion."[17] He noted also that he tried not to talk too much as he thought this put off his students and encouraged passivity. Professor Mary Harvey Doyno of the Humanities and Religious Studies Department at Sacramento State University begins class by speaking a little too loudly, trying "to pull the students out of their technology" and asks "general questions like how people are doing," and sets immediately to work learning names.[18] Paul Rahe of Hillsdale College invokes the "stern Paideia" in his Roman history classes. He likes to start with forbidding statements about student obligations and the difficulty of assignments. "Many are called, few are chosen." The intention is to chase away nonserious students and make clear to those who stay that the summer vacation is truly over. My Africanist colleague at Vanderbilt, Moses Ochonu, begins his survey course with a short video highlighting the popular stereotypes of Africa and Africans. He follows with a discussion exploring the stereotypes, seeking to replace them with an awareness of the "multiple constructed and reconstructed meanings" of Africa.[19]

Providing a clear outline of course goals is the constant here. Whether sternly stated or not, it is the surest way to set a course on the right path. Our biorhythms wax and wane, we are cogent, perhaps brilliant one day and disorganized and obscure the next. The well-conceived outline allows for the inevitable bad days we all have – the ones that make us want to quit.

---

16 Dana Goldstein, *The Teacher Wars: A History of America's Most Embattled Profession* (New York: Anchor Books, 2014), pp. 248–250.
17 Interview with Steven Epstein.
18 Mary Harvey Doyno, Where in the text? *Common Knowledge* 23:1 (2017), p. 3.
19 Interview with Moses Ochonu.

It is not a road map to sure success but it avoids a basic obstacle to effective teaching: lack of understanding by the students of what is expected of them by the professor. The flaw is fatal. Students first and foremost, as Wilbert McKeachie emphasizes in *Teaching Tips*, project themselves into the course via the syllabus, which should make clear the responsibilities and, at its best, engage students' imagination We shall speak in greater detail about this in Chapter 3.

A consistent question is how prepared is prepared? How detailed must I be? A colleague of mine cites the "Heisenberg principle" of teaching. When she tries too hard to organize every detail in advance, she invariably squeezes the life out of the class. When she is too loose, she has trouble connecting the parts and feels the course is not sufficiently coherent. Another colleague arranges his whole class around a very small, carefully chosen set of questions, based solely on the reading. He begins calling on the students the first day, to make the point that they must always be prepared. The practice allows him also to learn their names early, which helps invest the students in the course. The National Council for History Education suggests crafting "instructional activities" that present various points of view on historical issues and interrogates sources.[20]

Different professors have different guiding principles. Samantha Kelly, who teaches medieval and early modern Italy at Rutgers University, stresses the importance of assigning numerous brief writing assignments tied directly to the readings. They keep students engaged, facilitate daily discussion and provide numerous grades so that no single one will determine their final mark.[21] I employ a similar strategy but combine small and longer assignments and stress at each turn how the readings relate to the basic themes of the course. A book as seemingly distant from their ordinary lives as Augustine's *Confessions* can deeply resonate with students. The basic themes – "Who am I, and why is there evil in the world?" – are timeless. Anthony Molho, a historian of medieval and early modern Europe at Brown University and the European University Institute in Florence, keeps his weekly reading load light. He believes that "big and complex books" need to be read slowly and carefully and with close supervision by the instructor. Richard Davis, a historian of India at Bard College, is keenly aware that his students come to his class with little background in the subject, so he relies on a small set of carefully chosen primary texts, like the Bhagavad Gita, which have strong human appeal.[22]

---

20 National Council of History Education. NCHE Expectations for Teacher Preparation Programs. Best Practices of Teachers. www.nche.net/bestpracticeshisttchng
21 Interview with Samantha Kelly.
22 Interviews with Anthony Molho and Richard Davis.

The common element is, as scholars of pedagogy argue, to formulate clear learning objectives that can be assessed throughout the semester and involve close examination of sources.[23] For me, this involves an ongoing process of self-reflection: what are the things we want to accomplish, are we accomplishing them, and how can I better insure that we do? All practices flow from the course objectives and a mutual sense of discovery and critical engagement with texts. I make no effort to impress, but rather judge all activities in terms of pedagogical efficacy. Indeed, I offer an extra class to review for exams and papers, which students see as an act of generosity but is actually a self-serving deed, intended to lure students into devoting extra time to collective study; given the stakes, it focuses their attention and allows an intense discussion of critical assessment of sources and historical thinking. The goal is to use the "oppression" of tests and papers as a teaching tool.

Most professors view the first day of class as crucial. It is then that they lay down basic rules of the course, at a time when student attention is best. Some professors dismiss the students early, once the course objectives have been stated and the introductions are made. Others keep students for the whole time. Ernest Hartwell, writing in the pedagogical Dark Ages (1913), made sure that the first day of class was a particularly "heavy workday," to eliminate what he called the "inertia" of the summer. Caroline Walker Bynum seeks to deliver "a jolt" to students in the first meeting of her class on devotional objects, to force them to think about how political and social structures condition who makes objects and who controls and consecrates them.[24] She points out that using the first class effectively is challenging at Princeton, where she taught the course, because of the so-called "shopping" period, which allows student to come and go while the professor presses forward trying to ignore the ebb and flow (was it something I said?).

I am an advocate of the jolt to eliminate summer inertia. I purposefully use every minute of the first class, and even go a minute or so over. My aim, apart from making clear the course themes and getting to know the students, is to take full advantage of their undivided attention. The intention is also to make the subliminal point that every minute counts. I carefully explain my syllabus, which is thematically circular, beginning where I ultimately intend to end. Amy Remensnyder at Brown University starts the first day of her survey class on medieval Europe with a year in which nothing happened. Her purpose is to reinforce the reality that in

---

23 Laurie Richlin, *Blueprint for Learning: Constructing College Courses to Facilitate, Assess, and Document Learning* (Sterling: Stylus Publishing, 2006), pp. 6–8.
24 Caroline Walker Bynum, Where in the Text Symposium: In the Humanities Classroom. *Common Knowledge* 23:1 (2017), p. 68.

the Middle Ages, as in history more generally, most years were in fact of little obvious importance. I have stolen this for my own medieval courses.

For the first meeting of my Western Civilization class, I play a historiographical game. I critique "old-school" pedagogy. I place on the board (if I have one, otherwise I use a computer) at the beginning of class, without comment, a list of dates – 399 BCE, 330 CE, 476, 800, 1066, 1215, 1348, 1517, etc. I leave them up as I then talk about the readings and broader themes that we will examine. I turn then to the dates and ask the students if they can identify them. They usually guess several, particularly those relating to English history. I tell the students that this is how I learned Western Civilization in the old days, according to dates (I actually did not take Western Civ as an undergraduate), and how they will *not* learn it. We then talk about what the dates represent, what historical patterns they convey. Is it the lives of great men? Is it important political, religious, and economic events?

I do this to underline the fact that, then as now, historians make conscious choices about how they slice up history. And even something so seemingly empirical as a date reveals subjective judgments embedded in our craft; 1348 highlights the role of disease (the Black Death) as a historical force; 399 BCE (death of Socrates) privileges the role of philosophy and the great man.[25] History is constructed by historians, as are classes in the subject. I then ask the students to identify the events they would stress if asked to write a history of the world they live in. What issues define their age? The discussions have worked well, and are particularly useful for Western Civ, which has, more than any other course I teach, the stodgy air of old school "facts first *auctoritas*" (see Chapter 3). My students come expecting to learn the canonical facts, ones already settled upon, that they can draw upon later, often for no greater motive than to appear to be not entirely ignorant of the past. I want them to know that those facts and how they are arranged are subject to debate.

Doctors and Morticians

Who then is the good teacher? The answer is variable. Ernest Hartwell imagined the successful history teacher as someone who was "pedagogical and practical," "scholarly without being musty," "imbued with the love of his subject" and "familiar with human experience."[26]

---

25 William Caferro, Teaching Western Civilization. *Common Knowledge* 24:3 (2018), pp. 366–374.
26 Ernest Hartwell, *The Teaching of History* (Boston: Houghton Mifflin, 1913), p. 1.

The judgment is strikingly similar to that of Peter Filene, writing nearly a century later in 2005 (without reference to Hartwell), who likewise stressed the basic importance of the human element.

But understanding "human experience" would appear the most problematic requisite. The meaning and importance are intuitively clear. It helps to know humanity in order to teach human beings. Precisely what human experience, however, do we need to know and how do we hope to apprehend it from the vantage of our lofty ivory towers? The principal I worked for in secondary school approached the question by dividing teachers into two categories: "morticians" and "doctors." He asked a rhetorical question of all new faculty: "Are you a mortician or a doctor?" I was nonplussed when he asked me, having no idea what he was talking about. But luckily he supplied his own answer. Good teachers are doctors. They think of ways to make their patients (students) better. Bad teachers are morticians. They condemn student flaws and study habits, sometimes even cite an existential "downfall of humanity" in recent years. They pronounce the patient/student "dead on arrival."

This morbid metaphor has the benefit of reducing pedagogical experience to its simplest elements. Even if we do not understand the patient as a person, we may still devise ways to treat her/him. My own experience has in fact been that my students, despite their entirely different cultural reference points and increasing distance from my own world, do not seem so different from me, my friends and fellow students at their age. And I say this having taught in several places, including New York City, Connecticut, Oklahoma, and Tennessee. Where there is a basic desire to learn and to think, there is the possibility of a connection. The desire "to know" is the human element that ties us all together and does not end when formal classroom education stops, but follows us throughout our lives.

Nevertheless, history as a teaching field presents its own unique challenges in tapping into human experience. We do not teach science, whose importance is well understood by undergraduates even if they sometimes find it dry and difficult. The study of history does not lead directly to a postgraduation job, which has increasingly become a basic expectation at universities nowadays. History needs to be sold, and not only to the students and (by extension) their parents but also to universities as well (see Chapter 2). Anthony Grafton, a historian at Princeton University and recent president of the American Historical Association, argued in his essay "History under attack" (2011) that the "austere principled quest for knowledge" intrinsic to the study of history mattered all the more in the "current media world." But he admitted it is a "quest without a Grail."[27]

---

27 Anthony Grafton, History under attack. *Perspectives on History* (2011). www.historians. org/publications-and-directories/perspectives-on-history/january-2011/history-under-attack

Teachers of history courses look for a hook to tie their students to the material. Peter Allitt in his courses on recent American history wants his students to feel the "contingency of history" and how they are themselves connected to the changes in American since the nineteenth century.[28] Several of my colleagues in modern European history give assignments that require students to interview their grandparents or other members of the family or friends who have experienced an "historical event" of interest or can speak of a bygone era.

Not all of us are able, however, to find such contingency and immediacy, especially those of us who teach more distant eras and places. America had, for example, no medieval past, which means at base that the way medievalists teach the subject in this country is different from how they teach it in Europe, where the physical monuments of the era remain visible and medieval precedent is still drawn upon by public officials. Therefore, although it is excellent pedagogy to stress the currency of the past in the present world we live in, it is not necessarily always an option or, to be more precise, a desirable option.

Many professors seek deeper human connections (see Chapter 2). Richard Davis in his class on "Devotion and Poetry in India" at Bard College takes as his basic pedagogic goal to get his students, who are unfamiliar with the sources he assigns, to "enter into a subjectivity that is different from their own and challenges their values," but is at the same time "human and sympathetic."[29] Hoyt Tillman, a historian at Arizona State University, finds relevance for his survey of premodern Chinese history in the terrorist strike of 9/11 on America. The event serves as an entrée into a discussion of the relationship between executive power and individual rights/civil liberties, which he sees as central to understanding premodern China. Tillman evokes "historical empathy" from students to create a bridge for a more open dialogue about the challenges faced in the past. Wendy Doninger, a historian at the University of Chicago, finds that the Sanskrit texts she studies and teaches resonate also with students because "authors cared then about things that humans care about today: love, sex, death and fear."[30]

What is perhaps most difficult for historians of distant times and places to convey to students is their love of the unknown and unfamiliar, which often includes interest in foreign languages and paleography that drew them to the fields in first instance. Remoteness has its own intrinsic

---

28 Peter Allitt, *I'm the Teacher, You're the Student* (Philadelphia: University of Pennsylvania Press, 2005), pp. 2–3.
29 Richard Davis, Bhakti in the classroom: what do students hear? *Common Knowledge* 2 (2017), pp. 1–2.
30 Interviews with Hoyt Tillman and Wendy Doninger.

appeal, and may indeed be said to represent another aspect of the human condition. Human beings have always traveled far and wide to see things that are new and different, and to try to connect with people from other cultures. That which is strange or unusual can be used to strike a resonant chord with students who, like their professors, are attracted to the transformative dimension to education, which allows them to enter worlds previously unknown. The visual and tactile aspects of documents and old books can now, via the internet, be brought before the students in ways previously unavailable (see Chapter 4).

The medievalist Marc Bloch, a founder of the famous Annales school of historical study, addressed the issue of history's appeal in the middle of the twentieth century. He argued that the chief value of history is its ability to capture the imagination and "to entertain." He asserted that from a "simple liking" evolves a more general "yearning for knowledge."[31] The eighteenth-century philosopher David Hume argued similarly, adding, however, a more explicit moral component: "The advantages found in history seem to be of three kinds: as it amuses the fancy, as it improves the understanding and as it strengthens virtue." He added that history opens the door to other "parts" of knowledge, "extends our experience to all past ages," to distant nations, which ultimately improves "our wisdom."[32]

We shall speak more about these issues, in historical perspective, in the next chapter but the notion of "amusing the fancy" should not be casually dismissed. The church father Augustine of Hippo made essentially the same point in his *Confessions*, admitting that he "hated Greek literature" because he feared punishment from his teachers, but he loved Latin because he was "encouraged by jokes and laughter." "I learned Latin not under pressure, but by my own heart." For Augustine, this was proof that "unbridled curiosity" was the most effective pedagogical tool.[33] Indeed, the methods underlined by Augustine follow closely modern pedagogical notions of "student-based" learning. And once it becomes fun, it becomes part of who we are.

Augustine's dislike of Greek would have important consequences for western Christendom. It denied him – and the West – access to the Greek Christian heritage and the original language of the Gospels. But to our present point, the line between pleasure and pain is blurred. Education is most effective when it is fun but teachers must also be demanding and exacting in their daily requirements. In a treatise on education written

---

31 Marc Bloch, *The Historian's Craft* (New York: Alfred A. Knopf, 1953), p. 7.
32 David Hume, Of the Study of History (1741). In: *Essays, Moral, Political and Literary*, edited by Eugene F. Miller (Indianapolis: Liberty Fund, 1984).
33 Augustine, *Confessions* (New York: Everyman, 1907), pp. 20–21.

back in fifteenth-century Italy, Pier Paolo Vergerio asserted that "good results" could only be achieved if the student was willing to be "criticized and chastised." "It is seemly to endure abuse," Vergerio wrote, "as long as there is not too much severity." [34] The advice was intended for the male children of the aristocratic elite and addressed specifically to the son of Francesco Carrara, lord of Padua. In the early twentieth century, Abraham Flexner, founder of the Institute of Advanced Study and author of a comparative history of universities, stated that college education should create "a crisis" among students that "is ultimately for the greater good." [35] The American college students about whom Flexner spoke were not dissimilar to those of Vergerio – male and from the elite.

In more recent years, Mark Bauerlein of Emory University, author of *The Dumbest Generation: How the Digital Age Stupefies Young Americans and Jeopardizes Our Future*, has advocated for a very different approach. He asserts that he used to be a "hard line, great books" advocate but came to believe that in the "age of Game Boy and Facebook," students deserve more discretion in choosing their own assignments. He found it acceptable for students to read "entertaining" books like Harry Potter, as long as faculty "preserve book reading habits."[36] I choose books that I think are enjoyable, with the awareness that what I think is fun may not be what the students think is fun. I believe, like Professors Bynum and Flexner, that a basic challenge for college teachers is to get students to appreciate what they may otherwise not read themselves. It may be that I have more faith than Bauerlein in the ability of students to read and develop intellectually on their own, to read their own favorite books in conjunction with those I am trained to teach. But as a colleague who teaches antiquity often reminds me, students still connect viscerally with Plato's dialogues and, indeed, he gets nervous assigning parts of Ovid's *Art of Love* because he does not feel sufficiently mature to handle the probing questions that will inevitably follow. I insist, as may be evident from the foregoing discussion, on teaching Augustine's *Confessions* wherever I am able because it is, at base, a book about a person trying to figure out who he is, contemplating the world around him and why there is evil in it. He is also a seminal figure of the period I teach, the Middle Ages, which may otherwise be appealing only for its "strangeness" – which, as noted above,

34 Pier Paolo Vergerio, The character and studies befitting a free-born youth. In: *Humanist Educational Treatises*, edited by Craig W. Kallendorf (Cambridge: Harvard University Press, 2002), p. 21.
35 Abraham Flexner, *Universities, American, English, German* (Oxford: Oxford University Press, 1930), p. 28.
36 Motoko Richaug, A new assignment: pick books you like. *New York Times* (August 29, 2009).

is nevertheless also an effective teaching tool. If I cannot sell Augustine to a group of young people, I think I should find a different line of work.

There is nevertheless sound pedagogy in all the above approaches. The choice of assignment must ultimately reflect the person who assigns it or, as Ken Bain asserts in his *What the Best College Teachers Do*, instructors must adjust their teaching to who they are. [37] If you enjoy teaching a topic, it is likely that the student will enjoy reading and learning about it. This may perhaps appear to be too reductive and roseate a view but even if the student dislikes the reading, the image of an engaged professor valiantly making his/her case is worth something in itself. Anthony Molho recalls how during lunch-time discussions among history faculty at a "grubby" cafeteria at Brown University known as the Gate, he and his colleagues, representing diverse subfields, found more similarities than differences in their approaches to teaching. They agreed that the discipline of history was sufficiently "capacious" to allow professors to "expand the conceptual terrain they considered appropriate to historical inquiry." They all shared the "element of time" as a fundamental component of their study.[38]

The point is worth stressing here because an unnecessary and largely generational divide has posited a fundamental unbridgeable opposition between student-centered and teacher-centered learning. Some recent authors have argued that teachers should abandon their own "peculiar enthusiasms" in favor of the perspective of a "bored student." The point is worthy, but teachers in my experience possess a basic empathy that inclines them to try to align their "peculiar enthusiasms" with the supposed boredoms of students. Indeed, to assume the perspective of a bored student is *prima facie* problematic, as it reduces students to a monolith and subverts a central purpose of learning: to force students out of their comfort zones and encourage true critical thinking. The "best teachers," Ken Bain found in his study, are those who treat pedagogical issues with the same intellectual rigor that they treat their research and who unapologetically expect more from students than they believe that they can handle.[39]

Imitatio as Innovatio

The challenges of the beginning teacher nevertheless remain the central issue here. Several colleagues stress the value of imitation in the early phases of their teaching careers. Hilmar Pabel, a professor of Reformation

---

37 Ken Bain, *What the Best College Teachers Do* (Cambridge: Harvard University Press, 2004), p. 100.
38 Interview with Anthony Molho.
39 Ken Bain. *What the Best College Teachers Do*, pp, 15–17, 21.

Europe at Simon Fraser University in Vancouver, tells how during the first years of his career he instinctively imitated his advisor, Jaroslav Pelikan of Yale University. He abstracted his early courses from Pelikan's syllabi, used similar readings and even found, when lecturing, that he sometimes spoke like his advisor, using a few noteworthy expressions – "hemi-semi-demi;" "whether he nailed them or mailed them, Luther nevertheless *posted* the 95 theses." Pelikan still occasionally reappears in his lectures. Indeed, I find Professor Pelikan in my own classes. Hilmar and I arrived at graduate school together and were both transfixed by Pelikan's wonderful lectures on the medieval Christian tradition East-West. We served several times as his teaching assistants. After a few years, it got so that we were able to imitate his inflection and tone. Hilmar did it better than I. "We may not be great historians," we used to joke, "but we can sound like one!"

The professor I most imitated when I first left graduate school was John Boswell, who had been my *de facto* advisor for most of my graduate career. I admired his meticulous organization, his choice of readings and his enthusiastic, learned, humorous, and empathetic presentation of material. He entered the classroom in a friendly, easy-going way – no pretense, comfortable with himself. The moment he started to speak, however, it was clear that he was an undisputed master, whose knowledge was forged at a high temperature. The subject matter seemed to speak through him, emboldening him, pushing him further on, challenging him as much as his listeners. This struck me to the core, and corresponded so well with my own attitude, both toward myself and toward the subject matter (and perhaps my otherwise complete lack of personal confidence). When I ultimately got my first full-time university teaching job, I offered a class called "Judaism, Christianity and Islam," the same one that I had taken and TAed for as a graduate student. I altered the readings but the main lines were very much the same.

Such blatant copying would get us all charged with plagiarism if it involved our written scholarly work. But imitation as a basic learning tool stands on firm pedagogical ground, and goes way back into the distant past. Giovanni Boccaccio transcribed the works of Dante and Petrarch in order to capture the spirit and style of their work. Petrarch in turn copied Cicero, and patterned his *Letters on Familiar Matters* on the personal correspondence he found by the Roman writer in a library in Verona in 1345. A basic feature of the never-ending debate about "the Renaissance" has been whether "imitation" of the ancients by humanist writers led to "innovation" and new ways of thinking or merely slavish devotion to precedent. As recent literature has argued, even if the intention is to faithfully follow our predecessors, it is unlikely that, mediated through our own persons, the message will remain unchanged.

With this in mind, one of our assignments for the graduate students in our teaching class at Vanderbilt is to have them observe professors and write a critique of their teaching styles. Students implicitly critique all their teachers but the explicit evaluation has the benefit of making them truly think about the craft. Students point out what they like and what they do not like. It is an awkward exercise both for them and the professor. Students feel uncomfortable with their openly evaluative comments, and the teacher of the course will hear things that she/he does not want to know about colleagues – members of the same guild for whom there is an inherent sense of solidarity. I confess that I wanted to eliminate the exercise from our syllabus, but colleagues convinced me otherwise and the practice is indeed fruitful.

The critique helps students see ways that they would put their own stamp on classes. They ponder closely what they believe would work for them, and implicitly how their goals differ from those of their professors. Interestingly, one of the main points of discussion in our seminar focused on "toughness." Some students found the professors they observed lacking in this regard, believing that they catered too much to student opinion. They also pointed out imprecise and clumsy use of technology (see Chapter 3), and saw organization, class management, intellectual engagement, and enthusiasm as keys to good pedagogy.

The exercise made equally clear that the images conveyed by one effective professor were not the same as those conveyed by another effective professor. The students saw distinctions along gender and racial lines, in terms of age, general bearing, and habits. The assignment reinforced the importance of reading faculty teaching statements that we asked them to do in our first meeting. It also made clear the gap between theory and practice, and with it the importance of Pirsig's motorcycle.

Casting Images

What emerged at base from the discussion is that whether or not we imitate our forebears, our reception in the classroom depends on variables that are not easily quantified. The goal is to transcend these things but the variables need to be explicitly acknowledged because they often are not.

It is also important to acknowledge that teaching also depends on the nature of one's students. And this depends also on the type and size of the course and the institution (see Chapters 2 and 3). Very large classes make intimate, lively exchange of ideas difficult. Very small classes can also inhibit discussion. Augustine of Hippo, a professor of rhetoric in the first instance, left his post at Carthage to go to Rome because he hoped that the students would be "quieter" and less inclined to "invade the lecture room" and "indulge in wild antics."[40]

Modern-day professors can relate. Teaching is inherently unstable because the object of our labor – even at the same school – does not remain the same. Thus, however much we prepare, it is not entirely clear how things will actually go. The skill level of students varies not only from school to school, but from class to class and even, in my experience, according to the time of day a class is taught.[41] Colleagues report that Friday classes are often "curiously" empty, especially as the semester proceeds. I have had less problem with those than with late afternoon classes, especially on a nice day.

The differences are nevertheless not always what one would expect. Jennifer Spock, a historian of medieval Russia, points out that while the students she teaches at Eastern Kentucky University are nontraditional and lack the skills of those she taught as a TA at Yale University, they "internalize information more strongly" and often discuss materials more enthusiastically and personally.[42] My students at the University of Tulsa, a commuter school, were often older, had gone to junior college first and worked for a time in the outside world to make the money to go to university. They were as a result often highly motivated and very appreciative. As a medievalist, I found that they knew the Bible – important to the study of my field – better than their counterparts up north, where I was a TA and adjunct (at Fairfield University, a Jesuit institution!). This owed in large part to the fact that many were from Protestant denominations where Bible study was common. At the same time, however, the course I stole from John Boswell on Judaism, Christianity and Islam took an unexpected turn in that same setting. In a fit of youthful exuberance, I grew a beard when I took the job at Tulsa. In combination with my dark completion (and teaching Surahs of the Koran), the students believed I was myself Muslim, specifically an Egyptian, as "Caferro" sounded to some of them like "pharaoh." I was informed of this by several colleagues and as a pedestrian Italian-America from New York City I was surprised, amused and pleased. I thought that the misidentification could be used to pedagogical advantage. It would make the class all the more meaningful if they accepted being taught from the "other" side.

The class did not, however, work, and it had nothing to do with misidentification. I am not John Boswell and did not have mastery of the material, and just did a poor job teaching it. But the experience was illustrative of the unexpected challenges that teachers face and the images we

---

40 Augustine, *Confessions*, pp. 96–97.
41 Laurie Richlin, *Blueprint for Learning*, pp. 13–17.
42 Interview with Jennifer Spock.

project. I taught that class back in 1994, and it coincided with the bombing of the Murrah building in Oklahoma City. I was in fact in class when the tragedy occurred and when I returned to my office, unaware of what had happened, I was confronted by an angry secretary, who blamed "my people" for the deed, which was in fact initially attributed to Islamic terrorists. Several faculty members quickly escorted me away before I could fully understand what she was talking about or indeed what had happened. I assumed that the reference to "my people" was to New Yorkers, whom no one loves anyway.

Signature Pedagogies and Historical Thinking

Whatever images we cast and however we go about our craft, the growing literature on pedagogy suggests that teaching history, like other subjects, has a strong disciplinary aspect to it and that the instruction students receive in high school is often fundamentally different from what is expected of them in college. The point is critical. Lee Shulman, the president of the Carnegie Foundation for the Advancement of Teaching, encouraged college teachers to use "signature pedagogies" for their fields, by which he meant approaches geared to their disciplines. The Carnegie Foundation sponsored a series of comparative studies that examined how the members of different professions (e.g., clergy, 2005; lawyers, 2007; engineers, 2008; nurses, 2009; and physicians, 2010) receive their training.[43] The studies revealed distinct disciplinary ways of thinking and instructing students. Sciences, for example, were more fact and textbook based, while the humanities were more ambiguous. The historian Lendol Calder interpreted "signature pedagogy" as avoiding the "facts first" approach of high schools in favor, in his American history survey, of "self-reflection." Self-reflection for Calder necessarily begins with the question "what is history?" and includes understanding that historical knowledge is "fraught" with difficulties.[44] The expert on pedagogy, Peter Seixas, advocates inculcating "historical consciousness," looking at cognitive and cultural factors that shape our understanding of the past and its relation to the present day.[45]

The approaches highlight a fundamental challenge facing college history teachers that beginners and seasoned veterans do well to acknowledge. Students enter our courses without proper understanding

---

43 Lee S. Schulman, Signature pedagogies in the professions. *Daedalus*, 134:3 (2005), pp. 52–59.
44 Lendol Calder, Toward a signature pedagogy. *Historical Survey*, pp. 1361–1363.
45 Peter Seixas, Centre for the Study of Historical Consciousness. www.cshc.ubc.ca/about/

of the kinds of reasoning required to think historically. The cognitive behavioralist Sam Wineburg has argued that the basic nature of the primary and secondary school curriculum makes it difficult for students to adapt to the discipline-specific forms of reasoning they encounter in college history courses. They are presented in the first instance with generic tests of reading comprehension and textbooks that present history like biology, language, arts, and other subjects. The footnotes and structure of historical evidence and argument are stripped away, erasing the "epistemological distinctions" that lie at the heart of the discipline. History is conveyed with "a single tongue."[46]

The attention to these issues demonstrates the progress made by professional historians in developing teaching philosophies and "critical reflection" of their craft. The notion of a "scholarship of teaching" has gained currency since 1990, when Ernest Boyer first popularized the term.[47] In addition to the Carnegie Foundation, important foundations such as the Pew Charitable Trust, the William and Flora Hewlett Foundation, the American Association for Higher Education, the Association of American Colleges and Universities, the Council of Graduate Schools and other professional organizations have launched initiatives designed to help professors advance scholarship about teaching their disciplines. These have been accompanied by journals – *Perspectives, Inside Higher Education, Innovative Higher Education, Chronicle of Higher Education, Journal of Excellence in College History, History Teacher*, among others – that relay pedagogical approaches and experiences of historians. There are in addition web pages including for teaching centers such as the Goldberg Center at The Ohio State University (http://goldbergcenter.osu.edu) and the Teaching Center at Vanderbilt, which post an array of the latest pedagogical approaches; the Roy Rosenzweig Center for Teaching and New Media, which has partnered with CUNY and the Smithsonian Museum to provide digital sources, the Historical Thinking Project (http://historicalthinking.ca) directed by Professor Peter Seixas of the University of British Columbia and the Stanford History Education Group (SHEG) (https://sheg.stanford.edu), led by Sam Wineberg, partnered with the Library of Congress, that has recently launched Beyond the Bubble (https://sheg.

---

46 Sam Wineburg, *Historical Thinking and Other Unnatural Acts* (Philadelphia: Temple University Press, 2001), p.5.

47 Ernest Boyer, *Scholarship Reconsidered: Priorities of the Professoriate* (San Francisco: Jossey-Bass, 1991); Mary Deane Sorcinelli, Advancing the culture of teaching on campus: how a teaching center can make a difference. *New Directions for Teaching and Learning*, 90 (2002), pp. 41–48; Alan Booth, Rethinking the scholarly: developing the scholarship of teaching in history. *Arts and Humanities in Higher Education* 3:3 (2004), pp. 247–266.

stanford.edu/history-assessments) which provides a wide range of sources in addition to strategies to better elicit historical thinking, assess historical learning and critical reading of sources.

It is this scholarship and awareness of the "distinctive" nature of historical thinking that Julia Brookins (May 2013) argues is now becoming an indispensable component of instruction of graduate students. The constraints of limited time and the burdens of publishing render such instruction difficult and require a basic creativity that is worth the effort.[48]

---

48 Julia Brookins, History learning and teaching in the graduate curriculum. *Perspectives on History* (May 2013), p. 1.

2

Teaching History

> It may seem that the past is by definition over, but the past is always changing because historians and the purpose of history are changing too… (Lynn Hunt, *Writing History in the Global Era*[1])

At the turn of the twentieth century, the "Committee of Ten" of the National Education Association (1893), headed by the president of Harvard University Charles Eliot, advocated the study of history on the grounds that it helped "broaden and cultivate the mind," "counteract narrow and provincial thinking" and encouraged citizens "to exercise a salutary effect on the affairs of their country."[2] In their recent *History Manifesto* (2014), Jo Guldi and David Armitage make a strikingly similar argument. They assert that history is the subject that best teaches the type of careful judgment and broad perspective needed in the public sphere by politicians and policy makers. Indeed, Guldi and Armitage argue that the study of history is more important today than ever, owing to the digital revolution, globalization, and the flood of "big data" that require sophisticated investigation of long-term patterns.[3]

The strident nature of the affirmations makes clear, however, that history as a topic of academic inquiry has long had an image problem. While states have traditionally set requirements for mathematics, science and literature, they have not consistently done so with respect to history.[4]

---

1 Lynn Hunt, *Writing History in the Global Era* (New York: W. W. Norton, 2014), p. 4.
2 Paul Gagnon, History's role in civic education: the preconditions for political intelligence. In: Walter C. Parker. *Educating the Democratic Mind* (Albany: State University of New York Press, 1996), p. 243. See also National Education Association, Committee of Ten (1893), pp. 166–167. https://books.google.com/books?id=PfcBAAAAY AAJ&pg=PA3&lpg=PA3#v=onepage&q&f=false
3 Jo Guldi and David Armitage, *The History Manifesto* (Cambridge: Cambridge University Press, 2014), pp. 1–10.
4 Sam Wineberg, *Historical Thinking and Other Unnatural Acts* (Philadelphia: Temple University Press, 2001), p. 5.

Teaching History, First Edition. William Caferro.
© 2020 John Wiley & Sons, Inc. Published 2020 by John Wiley & Sons, Inc.

The priority has been to encourage learning in the sciences, by use of such programs as STEM (science, technology, engineering, and mathematics), over that of the humanities. And when Barack Obama recently challenged American schools and students (March 2015) to move "from the middle to the top of the pack" in the next decade, he spoke specifically about science and math. "Science is more than a school subject, or the periodic table, or the properties of waves. It is an approach to the world, a critical way to understand and explore and engage with the world, and then have the capacity to change that world..."[5]

"I'm concerned about my legacy—kill the historians."

Source: David Sipress, *New Yorker* Magazine/Conde Nast.

If science allows us both to understand the world and to *change* it, what then is the use of studying history? The scholar Lynn Hunt, whose words open this chapter, asks precisely this "nagging" question. "What is history good for?" She suggests that the inherent mutability of the subject, with its changing purpose and new questions asked of it by new generations of scholars, requires constant reexamination and reinterpretation.

---

5 President Barack Obama, Speech, March 23, 2015.

The fight for the relevance of the field in American universities is in any case a very real one, and an unmistakable air of pessimism hangs over the profession at the present time. Marc Bloch's faith in history's entertainment value and precursor to greater yearning for knowledge is unfortunately insufficient to justify its place in university curricula. In *The Marketplace of Ideas* (2010), Louis Menand spoke of an "overall rationale" problem for the humanities.[6] A spate of recent books and essays decry the overall devolution of the university into "crass commercialism," with students and parents playing the role of skeptical consumers, seeking a proportional return on their expensive investment. A growing cadre of "empty suits" (professional university administrators) manage the show, while faculty become increasingly part-time employees.[7] Economic crises have increased the discrepancy between rich and poor institutions, a pattern with unfortunate parallels in American society more generally.

"Vocationalism," Philip Altbach argues in "Patterns of higher education development," has become the "hallmark of the university curriculum" over the last two decades, citing, among other things, the spectacular growth of community colleges and for-profit institutions.[8] The largest number of bachelors' degrees in the United States are currently conferred in the "practical" field of business (22%). Only 2% of degrees are in history.[9] And enrollments in history have sharply declined at many schools; Julia Brookens' study for the American Historical Association shows that from the academic year 2012–13 to 2014–15, student enrollment in undergraduate-level history courses declined at 96 of the 123 academic institutions surveyed. This statistical evidence supports anecdotal

---

6 Louis Menand, *The Marketplace of Ideas: Reform and Resistance in the American University* (New York: W.W. Norton, 2010), pp. 54, 62.
7 Derek Bok, *Universities in the Marketplace: The Commercialization of Higher Education* (Princeton: Princeton University Press, 2009); Jennifer Washburn, *University, Inc.: The Corporate Corruption of Higher Education* (New York: Basic Books, 2006); Frank Donoghue, *The Last Professors: The Corporate University and the Fate of the Humanities* (Bronx: Fordham University Press, 2008); Gaye Tuchman, *Wannabe U: Inside the Corporate University* (Chicago: University of Chicago Press, 2009); Amanda Goodall, *Socrates in the Boardroom: Why Research Universities Should Be Led by Top Scholars* (Princeton: Princeton University Press, 2009); Andrew Delbanco, *College: What It Was, Is, and Should Be* (Princeton: Princeton University Press, 2012).
8 Philip G. Altbach, Patterns of higher education development. In: *American Higher Education in the Twenty-First Century: Social, Political and Economic Challenges*, edited Philip G. Altbach, Patricia J. Gumport and Robert O. Berdahl (Baltimore: Johns Hopkins University, 2011), pp. 15–16, 26–27.
9 Louis Menand, *The Marketplace of Ideas*, p. 18.

evidence of history faculty who have witnessed declines, sometimes dramatic, in the enrollment in their courses.[10]

To understand better the issues of today, it is important – as is the basic inclination of historians – to look at the past. When John Higham wrote about the state of historical study in the 1960s, he found himself inevitably drawn to the early roots of the profession in America to find an explanation for the status quo.[11] Francis Oakley, former president of Williams College, took a similar approach when trying to understand the "crisis" in the humanities during the Reagan years in the 1980s, as did Gary Nash, who sought to explain the "cultural wars" arising from the attempt to implement a new curriculum for the teaching of American History in those years.[12] Frank Donoghue, in a deeply pessimistic assessment of universities and the humanities (2008), argued that the "cataclysmic crises" of today reflect a state of affairs that has long been true.[13]

What is clear in all cases is that teaching history, like history itself, is contextual. Professors are not only the products of their educational backgrounds, but are also products of the institutions in which they work. Menand's backward glance at American universities impressed upon him a deep-seated institutional "inertia" that made attempts at change inherently difficult. He compared such efforts to "riding a horse to the mall."[14] The president of Johns Hopkins University, William Brody, wrote caustically in 2008 that a person visiting a university classroom at the turn of the twentieth century was likely to see little change at the turn of the twenty-first.[15]

Brody's comments were intentionally hyperbolic. The classroom of the twenty-first century is not the same as its predecessor from 100 years earlier. Technology alone has changed things (see Chapter 4). Every

---

10 Julia Brookins, Survey finds fewer students enrolling in college history courses. *Perspectives on History* (September 2016) www.historians.org/publications-and-directories/perspectives-on-history/september-2016/survey-finds-fewer-students-enrolling-in-college-history-courses

11 John Higham, *History: Professional Scholarship in America* (Baltimore: Johns Hopkins University Press, reprint 1989), p. ix. See also *Higher Education Cannot Escape History: Issues for the Twenty-first Century*, edited by Clark Kerr, Marian L. Gade and Maureen Kawaoka (Albany: State of New York University Press, 1994).

12 Francis Oakley, *Community of Learning: The American College and the Liberal Arts Tradition* (Oxford: Oxford University Press, 1992), pp. 3–10; Gary B. Nash, Charlotte Crabtree and Ross E. Dunn, *History on Trial: Culture Wars and the Teaching of the Past* (New York: Vintage Books, 1994), p. xi; Joyce Appleby, Lynn Hunt and Margaret C. Jacob, *Telling the Truth About History* (New York: W. W. Norton, 1994), p. 5. The authors, writing in 1994, say that "rarely has history been such a subject of controversy."

13 Frank Donoghue, *The Last Professors*, p. 1.

14 Louis Menand, *The Marketplace of Ideas*, p. 17.

15 Quoted in Andrew Delbanco, *College: What It Was, Is and Should Be*, p. 18.

classroom at my university is equipped with a computer, which was not the case when I started my career. But the heritage of the American university does affect the way that knowledge is disseminated, the way that we teach and even the way we are received. And Hunt's question – "What is history good for?" – must be understood not only as a disciplinary one, but also a pedagogical one. The two are instrinsically linked even if they are not typically presented that way. There are unfortunately few studies that examine the *ways* in which history was taught over the long run. Nevertheless, close examination of discussions about the *utility* of history reveals embedded discussions about the manner in which the subject was taught. The connection is, however, camouflaged by the ubiquitous "state of the field" historiographical essays that give the status of research affairs at a particular moment, but say nothing about how the ideas are relayed in classes.

Menand isolates a basic and pressing pedagogical problem. How do today's professors adapt the "long held linear model of transmitting knowledge" to a "generation of students who are accustomed to dealing with multiple information streams in short bursts?"[16] Academic inertia meets the internet generation.

History and the American University: A Long View

It is important to stress from the outset that universities are among the world's oldest and most enduring institutions.[17] It is difficult to find an American corporation that is older than Harvard (1636), the country's first university, which predates the nation itself. For that reason alone, it is important to underline notions of inertia. The European university, upon which American institutions are based, goes back to the Middle Ages.[18] Some non-European universities are still older.[19]

And there are noteworthy similarities between the medieval genre and its modern American counterpart. Medieval universities had, like American ones, religious affiliations. Students came to school at a point

---

16 Louis Menand, *The Marketplace of Ideas*, p. 19; see also Sam Wineberg, *Why Learn History (When It's Already on Your Phone)* (Chicago: Chicago University Press, 2018).
17 Guldi and Armitage, *History Manifesto*, p. 5.
18 Samuel Eliot Morrison began his history of Harvard with a discussion of the Middle Ages and even compared medieval man to his "frontier" American counterpart. Samuel Eliot Morrison, *The Founding of Harvard* (Cambridge: Harvard University Press, 1935), pp. 6, 7.
19 Francis Oakley, *Community of Learning: The American College and the Liberal Arts Tradition* (Oxford: Oxford University Press, 1992), pp. 19–20.

of passage in their personal lives and pursued a curriculum focused on the arts ("the seven liberal arts"), intended to prepare them for professional and public service. Medieval students could specialize in law or medicine, two popular choices that were, as today, remunerative, although canon law was the better financial choice than civil law back then (resembling contemporary corporate law in that canon lawyers worked for the biggest corporation then, the church). Students came primarily from the middle level of society and often traveled long distances from home to attend university. Extant Goliardic literature – poems about drinking, gambling, and sex – suggest that medieval students behaved much the same back then as they do now. The twelfth/thirteenth-century French theologian Jacques de Vitri (d. 1240) gave an acerbic and all too familiar description of the state of affairs at his alma mater, the University of Paris, in the thirteenth century. "Some students studied merely to acquire knowledge; others to acquire fame; others still for the sake of gain … very few studied for their own edification, or that of others…" He spoke of internal dissensions and issued some striking regional stereotypes. The English were "drunkards," the French were "proud, effeminate and adorned like women." The Germans were "furious and obscene at their feasts," Normans were "vain and boastful." Lombards (northern Italians) were "avaricious, vicious and cowardly" and Sicilians were "tyrannical and cruel."[20]

The particulars differ, but prejudice and presumptions unfortunately still exist on college campuses today (see Chapter 5). The first American universities derived most closely from English precedents, rooted in the Middle Ages, but based on the experience of seventeenth-century Puritans at Cambridge and Oxford universities. Harvard's founding charter defined its purpose as promoting "knowledge and Godlyness" in young men.[21]

History was not a distinct field of study in the Middle Ages, nor did it exist in early American universities. It was subsumed under the rubric of general education, at whose core lay theology, which connected all intellectual endeavors. In this respect, the first American universities, current-day rhetoric notwithstanding, were more interdisciplinary than they are now. The mission of the early schools was, as the historian

---

20 *Translations and Reprints from the Original Sources of European History*, published for the Department of History of the University of Pennsylvania., Philadelphia, University of Pennsylvania Press (1897–1907), vol. II, pp. 19–20.
21 Roger L. Geiger, *The History of American Higher Education: Learning and Culture from the Founding to World War II* (Princeton: Princeton University Press, 2015), pp. 3, 7; Clark Kerr, *Uses of the University*, 3rd edn (Cambridge: Harvard University Press, 1982), p. 152.

Samuel Eliot Morrison wrote, "to develop the whole man" and make him more inclined to "gentility and public service."[22] The goal matches well with what would later become a basic rationale for the study of history. And "man" must be understood here in the literal sense, since only men (white men) went to medieval and early American universities.

Several constants emerge from the long view of American colleges and the study of history at them. First, history was always closely associated with personal development and civic duty. The meaning of the two is relative and has not remained the same over the years. Second, as historical research agendas developed, so too did the methods of historical instruction. The "facts first" approach, under virulent attack today and rendered more problematic by the advent of the internet, was in fact always problematic, albeit an ever-present occupational hazard. Third, the competition between history and other disciplines, notably science, is long-standing, as is the contest between "practical training" for a profession and "impractical" education for nourishment of the soul. Finally, students – the variable object of professors' labor – have always been a challenge to teach. Students at seventeenth-century Cambridge were, according to a contemporary account, given to "swearing, drinking and rioting."[23] An extant student diary from early twentieth-century Cornell reveals a young man's intention to take only "snap courses," easy classes with easy teachers, to earn "cheap" credits.[24] Meanwhile, the diary of a student at Princeton at about the same time tells of his inability to stop laughing in class because of the "funniest word" he had ever heard. The word was "Spinoza."[25]

The list is not inclusive but it serves as an entrée into our discussion. The first American universities had neither historians nor history departments. History writing was the privilege of wealthy white patrician men with the money and time. The contemporary historian Bonnie Smith describes the men as "jurists, bankers and bureaucrats," who wrote for an "unspecialized cultivated" audience.[26] The history profession was thus

---

22 Samuel Eliot Morrison, *The Founding of Harvard*, p. 37; Delbanco, *College: What It Was, Is, and Should Be*, p. 40.

23 Thomas Wentworth Higginson, *The Life of Francis Higginson* (New York: Dodd, Mead, 1891), pp. 11–12.

24 Laurence Veysey, *The Emergence of the American University* (Chicago: Chicago University Press, 1965), p. 273.

25 Craig Hardin, *Woodrow Wilson at Princeton* (Norman: University of Oklahoma Press, 1960), pp. 34–35.

26 John Higham, History: professional scholarship in America. *American Historical Review*, 100:4 (1995), p. 1; Bonnie G. Smith, Gender and Practices of Scientific History p. 1152.

born gendered, race and class based – characteristics that, as we shall see, have not disappeared but remain part of the field.

And history did not have a particularly good intellectual reputation. The English writer Samuel Johnson (d. 1784) believed that the subject did not require "imagination in any high degree" and compared it in that regard to the "lower parts of poetry."[27] The modern scholar Roger L. Geiger, who has studied the broad arc of American higher education, described early historical study as preoccupied with "dead languages" and ancient people with the intention of instilling "mental and moral discipline," which in turn developed a sense of "civic and Godly duty."[28]

A surviving course catalogue from the University of Pennsylvania in 1851 verifies this. To gain entrance into the school, students were required to pass exams in Latin and Greek. This involved translating passages from Caesar's *De Bello Gallico*, Virgil's *Aeneid*, Xenophon's *Anabasis* – tasks that correspond closely to the course of studies of a modern-day classics majors at most American universities. The faculty at Penn consisted of six men, two of whom were ordained ministers. There was no separate department of history, but rather a department of history and English literature. This was true also at University of Michigan, which was founded in 1841.[29] Yale and Princeton combined history with political science.[30]

The pairings are telling. They highlight the civic and human aspects of history teaching back then. Like literature, history relayed stories that cast light on human character, which helped people to better understand themselves. Like political science, history offered lessons that can be applied to the public sphere. As far back as 1403, the humanist Pier Paolo Vergerio, among the first to extol the virtues of history as a discipline (*On Noble Customs and Liberal Studies of Adolescents*), advised that the subject was best taught alongside moral philosophy. History provided "a cumulative wisdom" from the past. Moral philosophy served "to guide men's actions."[31]

---

27 Higham, *History: Professional Scholarship in America*, p. ix; *Boswell's London Journal, 1762–63*, edited by Frederick A. Pottle (New Haven: Yale University Press, 2004), p. 293. See also George H. Nadel, Philosophy of history before historicism. *History and Theory* 3 (1964), pp. 291–315.

28 R. L. Geiger, Ten Generations, p. 46.

29 Herbert Baxter Adams, *The Study of History in American Colleges and Universities* (Washington: US Government Printing Office, 1887), p. 89.

30 J. F. Jameson, The American Historical Review, 1895–1920. *American Historical Review* 26 (1920), p. 2.

31 Pier Paolo Vergerio, The character and studies befitting a free-born youth. In: *Humanist Educational Treatises*, edited by Craig W. Kallendorf (Cambridge: Harvard University Press, 2002).

It is not easy to assess accurately the effectiveness of teaching methods in the early American universities, owing to universal condemnations of them by later scholars, who describe the curriculum as "tedious," focused on "dull recitation" and matters of grammar. The American historian Richard Hofstadter, writing in the 1960s, called the early pedagogy "boring." He even blamed it for creating "tension and irritation" that led to bad student behavior.[32]

The course list from the University of Pennsylvania in 1851 shows that the school did indeed emphasize dead languages and ancient people. Historical instruction began with a class on the ancient world based on a textbook, Wilhelm Putz's *Manual of Ancient History and Geography*. Wilhelm Putz was neither a university teacher nor an American. He taught secondary school (*Gymnasium*) in Germany and his book, translated into English and annotated by Thomas Arnold, a professor at Trinity College in Ireland, was published in 1849. It was widely used in American universities and is completely forgotten nowadays.

Putz's book nevertheless provides insight into the pedagogy of early history classes. Putz began with a forceful and familiar statement about the utility of history. He argued that history "shines light" on "what we ourselves are doing every day of our lives."[33] He then stressed the importance of physical environment as a basic tool of historical analysis, an approach current in today's classes and in the scholarly literature more generally (see Chapter 4). One could properly understand ancient Greek city-states like Athens only if one understood the mountainous geography that relegated the city to a small urban space that facilitated personal interaction and encouraged expansion abroad. Putz started his historical narrative with Asia, which he called the "cradle of the human race" and "superior to all else in magnificence and wealth." He followed with a section on Africa and the ancient Egyptians and Carthaginians, and then moved to Europe and Greek and Roman civilizations. The last section is the longest because, as Putz says, modern society reflects the "intellectual, political and aesthetic ideals" of these people.[34]

Although Putz's perspective was clearly Eurocentric, it is noteworthy that he took a "world historical perspective" and steadfastly emphasized the "usable," often human lessons from the study of history. This is again familiar to modern classrooms. Herbert Baxter Adams, a university

32 Richard Hofstadter, The revolution in higher education. In: *Paths of American Thought*, edited by Arthur M. Schlesinger and Morton White (Boston: Houghton Mifflin, 1963), pp. 269–290.
33 Wilhelm Putz, *Manual of Ancient History and Geography* (New York: D. Appleton and Company, 1846), p. iii.
34 Wilhelm Putz, *Manual of Ancient History and Geography*, pp. 4, 5.

professor writing in 1887, tells us that Putz's book was, however, despised by students.[35] But Adams's younger contemporary, Abraham Flexner, founder of the Institute for Advanced Study in Princeton, argued forcefully for the subversive aspect embedded in Putz's approach. The study of "dead languages and ancient people," however dull and sterile they may appear, was, Flexner wrote, decidedly not sterile in the highly nationalistic context of the nineteenth century. "At first sight," Baxter wrote rhetorically," what can be more innocent than the resurrection of a dead language?"

> "But every time a dead language is exhumed a new nationality may be created. The humanist creates as well as solves problems. He helps free the Serbs and the Greeks from Turkish rule; he helps both to create and solve the Home Rule problem in Great Britain, stimulating self-consciousness in India, in Egypt and in China and among American negroes; he finds himself one of the causes of an exacerbation of nationalism and racialism which no one has yet learned to mollify or cure."[36]

Baxter's judgment, which provides also a panoramic view of the national and racial issues of the nineteenth century, is echoed by the report of the "Committee of Ten" of the National Education Association in 1893 cited at the beginning of this chapter. The committee urged professors to teach ancient history on the grounds that it revealed how the past continued to "live" in the present. The issues confronting the present day "were first recognized in Greece."[37] "Dead languages and people" had palpable relevance.

And indeed, similar justifications appear in textbooks used in today's history courses (particularly broad surveys). Study of the ancients is justified on the grounds that it provides insight into humanity. As noted in Chapter 1, many teachers of the distant past and ironically of non-Western topics often rely on such correspondences to appeal to students with little background in their fields.

The Big Bang and Professional History

The narrative of the study of history and American universities reaches a climax in the period from the last third of the nineteenth century to the decade after World War I. Scholars call this the "Big Bang" in US higher

---

35 Herbert Baxter Adams, *The Study of History in American Colleges and Universities*, p. 55.
36 Abraham Flexner, *Universities, American, English, German* (Oxford: Oxford University Press, 1930), p. 22.
37 *National Education Report*, pp. 174–175.

education.[38] John Higham described the transformation of the university in these years as "one of the most striking features of Western culture," comparable to the scientific revolution in altering "western thought and the modern mentality."[39]

The "Bang" reflected a growing America in terms of population, diversity, and wealth. Waves of immigrants doubled the nation's population (1870–1910); per capita wealth increased and the federal government expanded the public university system through a series of measures, most notably the Morrill Land Grant Act (1862), that brought agriculture and engineering into the college curriculum to serve a growing nation in need of these skills.[40] At the same time, universities also became "research" institutions, modeled on the German example of Wilhelm von Humbolt's university of Berlin (1809). Many American professors in fact received their advanced training in Germany. Daniel Coit Gilman went there as a student and transported the German system directly to Johns Hopkins University, which he founded in 1876, and devoted solely to graduate training. The era also saw the establishment of the first women's and black colleges, which thrived in the early twentieth century.[41]

The university system was opened to a broader range of students. Enrollment in colleges and universities more than doubled from 1919 to 1926. Faculty also increased but only by a third, making for a student to faculty ratio at US universities of 120 to 1 by 1926.[42] History departments now appeared as distinct entities, although they often consisted of only one or two faculty members.

From the point of view of teaching, the increase in the number of students and the slower rate of increase of faculty created the large lecture class, a feature of higher education that is still with us. Universities often preferred these type of classes, as today, for economic reasons. It was cost-effective to teach as many students as possible with as little manpower. Harvard became the first university to establish an elective system of classes that allowed professors to teach their own specialties and for students to choose their own course of study. Universities also adopted the

---

38 Louis Menand, *The Marketplace of Ideas*, p. 98; Walter Metzger, The academic profession in the United States. In: *The American Profession: National, Disciplinary and Institutional Setting*, edited by Burton R. Clark (Berkeley: University of California Press, 1987); Robert B. Townsend, *History's Babel: Scholarship, Professionalization, and the Historical Enterprise in the United States, 1880–1940* (Chicago: University of Chicago Press, 2013).

39 John Higham, *History: Professional Scholarship in America*, pp. ix–x.

40 Gary B. Nash, Charlotte Crabtree and Ross E. Dunn, *History on Trial: Culture Wars and the Teaching of the Past*, p. 32.

41 Laurence Veysey, *The Emergence of the American University*, pp. 158–163; Clark Kerr, *Uses of the University*, p. 18.

42 Robert Townsend, *History's Babel*, pp. 83–84.

German history seminar, popularized by the great historian Leopold von Ranke (1795–1886). It involved a small group of students working with primary source material and was intended for advanced undergraduate and graduate students.

From the perspective of history as an academic discipline, German methods encouraged "scientific methods of inquiry" which raised intellectual standards. The "jack of all trades" professor of the early days disappeared.[43] The PhD became a prerequisite for employment and required more rigorous study. Dissertations were longer, more sophisticated and intended for eventual publication as books by university presses that were also emerging at this same time. Scholarly research became the means for promotion. Academic ranks for professors were established in the 1890s.[44] The American Historical Association was founded in 1884, along with other professional organizations, including the American Association of University Professors (AAUP) in 1915 and the John Simon Guggenheim Foundation in 1925, which gave more research grants in history over the next decade than in any other field.[45] Flagship journals in historical subfields such as *Speculum* for medieval history and *Isis* for history of science appeared. The audience for historical works shifted. Scholars now wrote more for each other rather than for a patrician elite.[46]

The vicissitudes of the "Big Bang" period are worth relaying in some detail because the changes that occurred then still affect the academy today. The university shifted from a place devoted primarily to teaching to one designed primarily for research. In *History's Babel*, Robert Townsend argued that this "professionalization" of history caused an inevitable "fragmentation" into subfields, another distinguishing feature of today's academy (see Chapter 5).[47] The subfield of Latin America, for example, started at this time and functioned initially as a midway point between Europe and America. Interest in modern history grew at the expense of the "dead languages and ancient history" of the earlier years. The American Historical Association even called for more study of Asia and Africa, and a textbook, albeit an inadequate one, Carlton Hayes' *World History*, appeared in 1932.[48]

---

43 Laurence Veysey, *The Emergence of the American University*, p. 142.
44 John Higham, *History: Professional Scholarship in America*, p. 33; Veysey, *The Emergence of the American University*, pp. 176–177, 319–320; Clark Kerr, *Uses of the University*, p. 14.
45 Higham, *History: Professional Scholarship in America*, p. 31.
46 Robert Townsend, *History's Babel*, p. 92.
47 Townsend, *History's Babel*, p. 186.
48 Carlton Hayes, *World History* (New York: MacMillan Press, 1932).

The former president of the California state university system Clark Kerr referred to these new institutions as "multi-versities," on account of the fact that they offered a little bit of everything for students, including vocational training.[49] Abraham Flexner, who witnessed the changes first hand, complained forcefully about this. He accused universities of becoming "service stations for the general public."[50]

For all the diversity of choices, however, Lynn Hunt in *Writing History in the Global Era* makes the point that historical study remained essentially national in nature, aimed in the first instance at creating a national identity.[51] The goal corresponded with contemporary nationalist feeling in Europe and underlines the influence in America of German universities, where national unification was then occurring. The historical work of the great German philosopher Georg W. F. Hegel (1770–1831), with its grand narrative and emphasis on the centrality of the state, was popular in nineteenth- and early twentieth-century American classrooms. American notions of national identity were not only Eurocentric, but northern and western European-centric in particular. The Committee of Ten appointed by the American Historical Society in 1893 specifically recommended that American universities stress teaching English and French history. The former helped Americans understand problems of "local authority" and "the secret of constitutional government that lives in free states." The latter was necessary because France was quite simply the "leading nation in Europe from the twelfth to the eighteenth century" and "her history is... a history of civilization."[52] The chauvinism is apparent even in Carlton Hayes' *World History* textbook, which supposedly exposed students to the broader world. The author saw Africa as having little history of its own apart from European colonialism.

Robert Townsend has noted the negative consequences of the Big Bang for the art of teaching. He argued that it discouraged a dialogue on pedagogy, which became subordinated to scholarly agendas.[53] Lawrence Veysey argued similarly: professors put less emphasis on teaching and more on research. He attributed the basic distinction between "the two spheres" to this era.[54] Meanwhile, Larry Cuban, in an important

49 Clark Kerr, *Uses of the University*, p. 15.
50 Roger Geiger, The ten generations of American higher education, p. 56; Abraham Flexner, *Universities, American, English, German*, p. 45.
51 Lynn Hunt, *Writing History in the Global Era*, p. 2.
52 *National Education Report*, pp. 174–175.
53 Robert Townsend, *History's Babel*, pp. 117, 182.
54 Laurence Veysey, *The Emergence of the American University*, p. 144; Townsend, *History's Babel*, pp. 62–73.

study of secondary school education at the time, spoke of a deeply rooted "culture" of "stability" and resistance to new pedagogical learning techniques in that venue.[55]

But even if there is little evidence of an explicit dialogue among faculty about teaching, it would be wrong to assume that *de facto* experimentation with regard to methods did not occur. In his study of American colleges in 1887, Herbert Baxter Adams described the techniques used by professors at numerous schools, including at several of the new women's colleges – Wellesley, Smith, and Bryn Mawr. Adams focused on the actions of individual historians, who appear to have set the precedent at their institutions.[56]

The teaching methods that Adams relays are not unfamiliar to today's professors. He noted a tension between professors who favored lecture style, memorization, and the use of textbooks, and those who favored primary source reading and discussion. Adams himself preferred the latter. "No scrap book of fact can give wisdom any more than a tank of water can form a running spring."[57]

At Wellesley College, where the history department was first organized in 1877, Professor Mary Sheldon Barnes neither lectured nor used a textbook. She divided her classes into sections of twenty or fewer students and gave each a packet of original source material as weekly readings. She sent them to the library to consult illustrative maps and photographs.[58] Class time was devoted to discussion, based on students' notes on the reading. At contemporary Smith College, Professor Sarah Humphrey relied on a textbook, gave lectures and assigned independent reading (including Herodotus in the Rawlinson translation, still used today).[59] Humphrey set up a species of reserve reading to encourage her students to use the library.

To be sure, course study focused mostly on the ancient Greek and Roman civilizations. But teachers did then what teachers do today: they employed methods that were best suited to themselves and the institutions in which they worked. There was a measure of what scholars now call "place-based" learning, tailored to environment though not, so far as

55 Larry Cuban, *How Teachers Taught: Constancy and Change in American Classrooms, 1890–1990*, 2nd edn (New York: Teachers College Press, 1993).
56 Adams' examples lend some credence to William Clark's controversial assertion that the history profession was shaped in part by "charismatic" professors. William Clark, *Academic Charisma and the Origins of the Research University* (Chicago: University of Chicago Press, 2006).
57 Herbert Baxter Adams, *The Study of History in American Colleges and Universities*, pp. 34–35.
58 Adams, *The Study of History in American Colleges and Universities*, pp. 214–215.
59 Adams, *The Study of History in American Colleges and Universities*, pp. 176, 217.

one can tell, linked as today to entities outside the institution altogether. Sarah Humphrey used the library because Smith College allocated significant resources to its collection. Andrew White, who taught history at University of Michigan in the late nineteenth and early twentieth century, lectured to large classes in large university classrooms, befitting the behemoth size of the institution.[60] Mary Shelton Barnes' personalized packet of primary source readings has only recently been replaced by the internet.

Indeed, Herbert Baxter Adams' account makes clear that even though there was no scholarship on teaching or teaching centers then, historians gave significant attention to such issues.[61] It could not have been otherwise. The American Historical Association explicitly addressed classroom teaching in 1897. It endorsed the use of textbooks and of repeated drill, but it also made the forceful statement that history is not only "an accumulation of facts" but "a way of thinking and mental preparation to help face the challenges that citizens confront in their everyday life."[62] The statement mirrors that of Guldi and Armitage in their *History Manifesto* in 2014 and follows well the stated goal of historical study at Wellesley College at the turn of the twentieth century, which was "to provide students with enough information about the past to allow appreciation of its general development and characteristics" and "to think and feel historically."[63] The last statement stands at the core of cognitive behaviorist Sam Wineberg's work on teaching history that has been so influential in recent years, and on methods championed by an array of modern experts such as Bruce Sledright, Peter Seixas, and others.[64]

And like the present day, stark distinctions between "acceptable" and "unacceptable" teaching strategies miss the point. Andrew White preferred the stodgy approach of lecturing and memorization of historical facts, which, he argued, stood at the foundation of the discipline.[65] Herbert Baxter Adams nevertheless describes him as an effective and much-loved professor on account of his outstanding lecturing skill. At the same time, Francis Lieber, an historian at Columbia University, never

---

60 Adams, *The Study of History in American Colleges and Universities*, p. 99.

61 Adams, *The Study of History in American Colleges and Universities*, p. 222; Arthur M. Schlesinger, The history situation in colleges and universities 1919–1920. *Historical Outlook* 11 (1920), pp. 103–106.

62 Schlesinger, The history situation in colleges and universities 1919–1920, p. 61; Robert E. Keohane, The great debate over the source method, *Social Education* 13 (1949), pp. 212–218.

63 Adams, *The Study of History in American Colleges and Universities*, pp. 214–215.

64 Sam Wineburg, *Historical Thinking and Other Unnatural Acts*, pp. 5, 24.

65 Adams, *The Study of History in American Colleges and Universities*, p. 99.

lectured but used "terse and familiar language" to get his points across. He assigned fiction and poetry in the belief that they provided students with insight into how great writers portrayed the elements of character, which he saw as the most important aspect of historical understanding.[66] Lieber was also greatly admired by his students. And in an age before the internet and PowerPoint, Lieber engaged the visual media available to him. He used four blackboards at once, writing down concepts and words, familiar and foreign, to make clear their meaning.

The multiple blackboards still remain in many university classrooms as a physical vestige of the Francis Liebers of the past. But what Lieber did with the blackboards, many of us now do with a computer (see Chapter 4). And many present-day professors follow Lieber in assigning literature to reinforce history, aware that the line between the two disciplines is blurred. I have found that Umberto Eco's fictional *Name of the Rose* is more useful at getting at notions of medieval heresy than the historical sources I have used. When lecturing, I put key words and phrases (especially foreign ones) on a handout, to make it easier for students to follow. I took the practice from my own professors, who likely took it from their professors, forming perhaps an unconscious chain back to Lieber himself.

What is clear, then, is that the different approaches were not mutually exclusive. The key issue is the *manner* in which each approach was implemented. This is difficult to judge in historical perspective. If students emerged from class excited about the subject and eager to learn more, willing to interrogate source material and think critically, the preconditions for greater learning will have been met.

As Ken Bain reminds us, excellent teaching involves students leaving class wanting to learn more. And Raymond J. Shaw in a recent essay noted that in the current-day search for measurable learning goals, we must not ignore the immeasurable ones: the life revelations, transformations that may not manifest themselves until later but which alter the course of our life-long attitude toward learning.[67]

What is in any case evident is that notions of "the utility of history" were always writ large. As Arthur Schlesinger has argued, America's involvement in World War I inspired instructors to educate students to be "intelligent citizens of the republic and the world."[68] He credits the conflict with encouraging "innovation and experimentation" in the

---

66 Adams, *The Study of History in American Colleges and Universities*, pp. 69, 70.
67 Raymond J. Shaw, Assessing the intangible in our students (July 27, 2017). www.chronicle.com/article/assessing-the-intangible-in/240744
68 Arthur M. Schlesinger, The history situation in colleges and universities 1919–1920. *Historical Outlook* 11 (1920), pp. 103–108.

history curriculum.[69] Schools such as Ohio State, Iowa, Pittsburgh, Kansas, and Cornell began giving freshmen a choice of what history classes they could take. The most notable "innovation" was adoption of the course known as Western Civilization. The class derived from the Student Army Training Corps of World War I and first appeared (although there is some controversy about the issue) in 1919 at Columbia University with the title "Contemporary Civilization." The stated purpose was unabashedly patriotic. The course aimed "to educate young men on the causes of the war to help wartime morale."[70] Western Civilization offered what one skeptical scholar has called "European history with American relevance" based on the premise that North Atlantic nations and the United States were bound by a common history. The class was taught by textbook, James Robinson's *Introduction to the History of Western Europe*, which did much to encourage the mass market in such books that remains today. "From the First World War to the campus protests of the 1960s," wrote the historian Gilbert Allardyce, "all roads led to the Western Civilization class."[71]

It is important, however, to stress that as the civic utility of the discipline grew in importance, history remained a largely aristocratic and gendered pursuit. The goal of national service and the betterment of the individual was intended in the first instance for well-bred white men, who were still the most conspicuous element at universities. The board of *The American Historical Review*, the flagship journal in the field, consisted of "gentlemen of ancient stock," from England, Ireland, France, and Germany– what one recent scholar called a "homogeneous class with a common mission: to hinder the disorderly effects of immigration."[72] Henry Adams, a professor of medieval history at Harvard and president of the American Historical Association (in the late nineteenth century) and descendent of the famous Boston Brahmin clan, spoke for his generation when he called history "the most aristocratic of all literary pursuits, because it obliges the historian to be rich as well as educated."[73] The popularity of the German-style history research seminar helped raise intellectual standards, but it also encouraged, as Bonnie Smith has argued, the development of a male brotherhood and gendered pursuit of historical knowledge.[74]

---

69 Schlesinger, The history situation in colleges and universities 1919–1920, p. 108.
70 Nash et al., *History on Trial*, p. 51.
71 Gilbert Allardyce, The rise and fall of the Western Civilization course, *American Historical Review* (1982), p. 695.
72 John Higham, *History: Professional Scholarship in America*, p. 8.
73 Higham, *History: Professional Scholarship in America*, pp. 63–64, 70.
74 Bonnie G. Smith, Gender and practices of scientific history, pp. 11, 50.

Nevertheless, it is important to stress that history did not develop as a scholarly discipline in isolation. Arguments about its utility were then, as today, measured against the challenge of science. There was, to be sure, no STEM but Darwin's *On the Origin of Species* was published in 1859 and called into question the basic theological foundations that underlay American university education. It helped establish science as an independent part of the university curriculum.[75] History and science in fact developed concurrently in the academy and maintained an ongoing relationship that was often more supportive than confrontational. In his *Letter to American Teachers of History* (1910), Henry Adams argued that it was essential for historians to incorporate into their methodologies the recent work on the laws of thermodynamics.[76] Adams proclaimed that "physic-chemists and teachers of *Energetik*" had given new direction to historical studies, which, he added, "badly needs it."[77] It is not entirely clear what science Adams was talking about but he envisioned historians working closely with "departments of biology, sociology and psychology" toward a "common formula," to serve as a "working model for their study."[78]

Adams' ideas were unpopular with his fellow historians and, indeed, his book remains a curiously overlooked part of his overall *oeuvre* that includes his famous account of his own education (*The Education of Henry Adams*). But even if the particulars of Adams' argument were not widely appreciated, his insistence on the interwoven nature of historical and scientific study played an important role in the academy and has a distinctly modern analogue. Historians today often work closely with departments of biology, sociology and psychology, which appreciate the interaction. And as John Higham points out, science and history both grew greatly in stature during the world wars of the twentieth century. The basic goals of the two were strikingly similar: to foster knowledge for the betterment of the nation. Historians shared with scientists a fundamental belief in progress and objectivity. Indeed, historians saw their discipline as its own species of scientific inquiry, guided by empirical principles. Higham also points out that many scholars were attracted to the study of the history of science, which, along with military history, is the most deeply rooted of all subfields.[79] Historians saw both as "transnational" and "transformative," with the broadest possible relevance.

---

75 Andrew Delbanco, *College: What It Was, Is, and Should Be*, p. 76.
76 Henry Adams, *Letter to American Teachers of History* (Washington: J.H. Furst, 1910), p. 121.
77 Adams, *Letter to American Teachers of History*, p. 119.
78 Adams, *Letter to American Teachers of History*, pp. 203–204.
79 John Higham, *History: Professional Scholarship in America*, p. 47.

Meanwhile, "vocationalism" constituted a persistent challenge to the humanities. John Henry Newman's goal in his famous lectures on the British university system (*The Idea of the University*) was for students to seek knowledge for knowledge's sake.[80] But the Big Bang in university education in America coincided precisely with the rise of big business, which changed the economic and social landscape of America. The great captain of industry Andrew Carnegie despised the teaching of the humanities at universities. He believed that it prepared a person for "life on another planet" rather than success in current-day America.[81] The wealthy manufacturer of elevators, Richard Teller Crane, denounced the study of "impractical, specialized knowledge" such as "literature, art, languages or history" which he saw as holding little value in the real world.[82]

The issue played a prominent role in discussions about education at historically black colleges, which grew greatly after the Civil War. Booker T. Washington at the Tuskegee Institute in Alabama advocated notions of economic self-help through study of agricultural and industrial/vocational training. His contemporary, W.E.B. DuBois, stressed the need for a more elite and intellectual education ("Talented Tenth") to lead African-Americans out of economic, political, and social subjugation.[83]

The debate was forceful, and as the example of Washington and DuBois shows, the stakes were high and not entirely the same in the different contexts. Thorstein Veblen, known today for his concept of "conspicuous consumption" but also a professor and author of *The Higher Learning in America: A Memorandum On the Conduct of Universities by Business Men* in 1918, strongly defended Cardinal Newman's notion of "disinterested learning" and "the pursuit of intellectual enterprise with no pecuniary end."[84] Abraham Flexner went further, arguing that universities should banish all "technical, vocational and popular" education and the "practical importance" attached to the study of them.[85] It was, in any

---

80 "I am asked what is the end of University Education ... I answer that...it has a very tangible real and sufficient end, though it cannot be divided from that knowledge itself. Knowledge is capable of being its own end." John Henry Newman, *The Idea of the University* (Notre Dame: University of Notre Dame Press, 1982), p. 77.

81 J. Wall, *Andrew Carnegie* (Pittsburgh: University of Pittsburgh Press, 1989), pp. 835, 837.

82 Richard Teller Crane, *The Demoralization of College Life* (Chicago: H. O. Shepard, 1911), p. 5.

83 Frederick Dunn, The educational philosophies of Washington, DuBois, and Houston: laying the foundations for Afrocentrism and multiculturalism. *Journal of Negro Education*, 62:1 (Winter, 1993), pp. 24–34. W.E.B. DuBois, *The Talented Tenth* (September 1903) http://teachingamericanhistory.org/library/document/the-talented-tenth/

84 Thorstein Veblen, *The Higher Learning in America: A Memorandum On the Conduct of Universities by Business Men* (New York: B. W. Huebsch, 1918), p. 85.

85 Abraham Flexner, *Universities, American, English, German*, pp. 27–28.

case, the transformation of science into a remunerative professional career in the modern era – its development into a vocation – that made it an alternative to, and adversary of, the humanities as it is today.

Golden Age: Diversity and Stratification

The Big Bang in university development was followed by the so-called Golden Age (1945–75), during which universities underwent their greatest expansion.[86] The number of undergraduates increased by 500% and graduate students by 900% in these years.[87] More faculty were hired in the 1960s than in the previous 325 years of American higher education combined![88] The federal government invested increasingly large sums into the system. By 1988, the number of women (aged 18–24) enrolled in universities exceeded for the first time that of men, and nearly a fifth of college students were not white.[89]

These developments had important consequences for the study of history. Increased diversity on campuses helped broadened the topics of historical inquiry. Young history PhDs now came from disparate social and economic backgrounds and moved in new scholarly directions. Gary Nash spoke of "tectonic plate shifts" in history writing.[90] Peter Novick boasted of "great originality" among researchers, who uncovered "previously untold chapters of history."[91] Harvey J. Graff saw the "democratization" of historical inquiry, which produced a "great revision" in study.[92]

National history and the grand narrative gave way to social, cultural, and gender studies that better reflected the backgrounds of researchers. The hegemony of the "dead languages and ancient people history" was undone.[93] And as subfields multiplied, so did the types of history courses offered at universities.[94] The new courses brought calls for interdisciplinarity and greater attention to methodologies used in nonhistorical

---

86 Louis Menand, *The Marketplace of Ideas*, pp. 63–64.
87 Roger Geiger, The ten generations of American higher education. In: *American Higher Education in the Twenty First Century*, edited by Albach, Berdahl and Gumport, p. 61.
88 Louis Menand, *The Marketplace of Ideas*, p. 65.
89 Appleby, Hunt and Jacob, *Telling the Truth About History*, pp. 1–2.
90 Nash, *History on Trial: Culture Wars and the Teaching of the Past*, p. 52.
91 Peter Novick, *That Noble Dream: The Objectivity Question and the American Historical Profession* (Cambridge: Cambridge University Press, reprint 1991, published originally in 1988), p. 585.
92 Harvey J. Graff, Teaching and historical understanding: disciplining historical imagination with historical context. *Interchange* (1999), pp. 280, 283.
93 John Higham, *History: Professional Scholarship in America*, p. 52.
94 Novick, *That Noble Dream*, p. 578.

fields. Historians made use of social and anthropological theory, adding layers of sophistication to historical thinking. Collaborations such as the "Amherst Project" (1959–1972) made more available primary texts, including contradictory accounts of the same event.[95] Meanwhile, the PhD became correspondingly more demanding, involving mastery of a larger and more diversified secondary literature.[96] Ernest Boyer of the Carnegie Foundation described the period succinctly as a "revolution of rising expectations" in graduate study.[97]

These were good times for history as a discipline of study at universities. It became a prominent and popular part of university curricula. The British historian G. R. Elton, writing in 1967, saw the discipline as having all "the marks of a runaway boom."[98] But the boom came with challenges. The "universal" nature of historical study at early universities was now gone, replaced by what some complained was a lack of "cohesion" and an "absence of consensual agendas."[99] Richard Hofstadter argued that the "under-specialized" historian of yesteryear gave way to an "overspecialized" modern counterpart. And although higher education became more inclusive, the professoriate became more professionalized and thus correspondingly more hierarchical (see Chapter 5). Despite claims of interdisciplinarity, the evidence suggests that professors were often more dissociated from each other than ever. Clark Kerr famously remarked in 1963 that universities had become little more than "a series of individual faculty entrepreneurs held together by a common grievance over parking."[100]

Lack of cohesion presented problems not only with parking but also with pedagogy.[101] Some historians continued to work within frameworks laid down by the previous generation, while others undertook new approaches in conscious opposition to the past. The generational divides that characterized American politics in the 1960s and 1970s played themselves out in university classrooms. Opinions about what constituted effective classroom teaching were more polemicized, contentious, and entirely too personal. They were exacerbated by the fact that history retained its class, gender, and racial bias. In 1962, the president of the

---

95 William Weber, The Amherst Project and reform of history education. *History Teacher* 51 (November 2017).

96 Novick, *That Noble Dream*, p. 581.

97 Ernest L. Boyer, *Scholarship Reconsidered: Priorities of the Professorate* (Carnegie Foundation for the Advancement of Teaching, 1990), p. 11.

98 G. R. Elton, *The Practice of History* (London: Blackwell, 1967), p. 3.

99 Novick, *That Noble Dream*, p. 579.

100 Quoted by David W. Burr in "Is university parking a common grievance" (September 2011) https://www.parkingtoday.com/articledetails.php?id=1072

101 Peter Novick, *That Noble Dream*, pp. 578.

American Historical Association, Carl Bridenbaugh, likened the demographic shift in the profession to a "great mutation." In a now infamous speech at the annual AHA convention (29 December 1962), Bridenbaugh complained about the "urban" backgrounds of many of the young members of the profession that made them "outsiders to the American past," more interested in their homelands and the traditions of their parents. The new generation was "outer-directed," while Bridenbaugh saw himself as "inner-directed." He claimed that the study of history had changed so much that "it now appears probable that mid-nineteenth-century America or Western Europe had more in common with fifth-century Greece than with their own projections into the middle of the twentieth century." [102]

Bridenbaugh's statements helped fuel the now infamous "cultural wars" of the 1980s and 1990s. Historians (mostly Americanists) passionately debated the purpose of history, particularly its civic role. Self-appointed guardians of the western canon such as Allan Bloom (1985) and Roger Kimball (1995) denounced the "cultural relativism" of "tenured radicals," whose ideas threatened the basic fabric of the American republic (see Chapter 1).[103] They decried the development of a "political correctness" that undermined what they perceived as the basic purpose of a liberal arts education. Gertrude Himmelfarb (1987) faulted historians for focusing on "non-rational structures" and ignoring the basic facts of political history.[104] Spirited defenses were mounted by scholars such as Gary Nash, who took on right wing political ideologues like Lynn Chaney, who called for an end to funding for the teaching of histories steeped in the misbegotten "cultural turn."

Community College

Unfortunately lost in the debate was a concurrent "institutional turn" that was critical to teaching history. The multiculturalism of the Golden Age coincided with the dramatic growth of community colleges, which became a prominent force in historical education that is still more vigorous today. The two-year institutions (which continue to get short shrift

---

102 Carl Bridenbaugh, The Great Mutation. *American Historical Review* 68:2 (January 1963), pp. 315–331.
103 Allan Bloom, *Closing of the American Mind* (New York: Simon & Schuster, 1987); Roger Kimball, *Tenured Radicals: How Politics Has Corrupted Our Higher Education* (Chicago, Ivan R. Dee, 1990).
104 Gertrude Himmelfarb, *The New History and the Old* (Cambridge: Harvard Press, 1987), p. 6.

in the discussion of higher education) serve as an emblem of the intellectual and social stratification of the academic landscape and of current-day America.[105]

Community colleges are a product of the Big Bang era, created with the explicit intention of segregating the unwashed masses from the elite. The president of the University of Chicago William Rainey founded the first junior college (1901) in order to offer education to "lesser" students so that he could insulate his beloved university from those same students. Community colleges grew greatly during the Golden Age, owing to several initiatives, especially President Harry S. Truman's Commission on Higher Education (1947), which sought "to make higher education less an instrument for producing an intellectual elite" and more a "means by which every citizen, youth, and adult, is enabled and encouraged to carry his education … as far as his native capacities permit."[106] From 1945 to 1975, 657 two-year schools opened, more than had altogether existed to that point.[107] There are now 1116 community colleges overall in the USA, educating more than half the nation's undergraduates!

Community colleges are the moving image of multiculturalism. Charging a fraction of the tuition costs of elite colleges, the two-year institutions attract culturally diverse, nontraditional students, many without basic reading and writing skills, who often have families and full-time jobs. They reveal little about the research agendas of historians but numbers alone make clear their critical role in the development of pedagogy and expose the institutionalization of a disquieting disequilibrium in that regard. PhDs trained in the same manner and at the same research institutions as their counterparts at elite four-year colleges fill these jobs, which involve the most challenging teaching assignments. A recent essay in the online journal *Slate* calls this "the academy's dirty secret." Eight elite universities account for roughly half of all the history professors working in the USA, including at community colleges.[108] Faculty are thus not prepared for the additional burden, which will include teaching outside their scholarly fields and numerous and diverse general surveys. In this regard the community school professor bears strong resemblance to the universal history teacher of the mid-nineteenth century – without the aristocratic privilege.

---

105 Frank Donoghue, *The Last Professors*, p. 22.

106 Boyer, *Scholarship Reconsidered* (San Francisco: Jossey-Bass, 1991), p. 11. See also Richard L. Drury, Community colleges in America: a historical perspective. *Inquiry*, 8:1 (Spring 2003.)

107 Louis Menand, *The Marketplace of Ideas*, p. 67.

108 Joel Warner and Aaron Clauset, The academy's dirty secret. *Slate* (February 23 2015). www.slate.com/articles/life/education/2015/02/university_hiring_if_you_didn_t_get_your_ph_d_at_an_elite_university_good.html.

As they have institutionalized the disparities in American society, community colleges have allowed elite four-year colleges to continue to draw from the same elite pool of students. Given the often large size of their student bodies and their limited resources, students do not readily receive the close attention they do at small four-year institutions. The advent of online and for-profit universities in the 1990s has further altered the playing field. The majority of history teachers at these universities are hired on a part-time basis, prompting the *Journal of the Association of American Colleges and Universities* to speak of the "adjunctification" of higher education.[109] David Staley and Dennis Trinkle have compared present-day higher education to the American restaurant market. The choices range from "gourmet five star restaurants to fast food vendors."[110] Nevertheless, junior colleges have been at the forefront in technological innovation and are sites of some of the most deep-rooted teacher dedication, that has produced innovative teaching, which we will discuss further in Chapter 4.

Crises, Transformations, and Legacies of the Past

The assessments of recent critics of higher education border on the apocalyptic. They speak of "the steady decline" of the university since the Golden Age and the continuation of a long-term job crisis for history PhDs.[111] Federal funding for the humanities has become increasingly competitive and scarce. The recession of 2008 struck hard, particularly at poorer universities, and served to increase the stratification between the "haves" and "have nots." Enrollments at community colleges grew by 16% in 2008 and by double digits in 2010–11, while those at four-year schools fell.

There was also crisis within the history discipline itself. The field moved into still more "troubling" directions. Social-theoretical approaches gave way to questions about the historical process itself. Postmodern and post-structural analyses called into question the veracity of broad historical patterns and the ability of scholars to get at the truth. The vocabulary of the humanities shifted from the use of words like "objectivity, reason and knowledge" to terms like "interpretations, perspectives and

---

109 Philip W Magnuss, For-profit universities and the roots of adjunctification in US higher education. *Liberal Education*, 102:2 (Spring 2016).
110 David Staley and Dennis Trinkle, The changing landscape of higher education. *Educause Review* (2011), p. 8; James V. Koch, The multifurcation of American higher education. In: *The Future of Higher Education*, edited by Gary A. Olson and John W. Presley (Boulder: Routledge, 2009), p. 27.
111 Louis Menand, *The Marketplace of Ideas*, pp. 61–92.

understanding."[112] A basic question was whether indeed we could speak at all of meaningful historical patterns.

"Stat rosa pristina nomine, nomina nuda tenemus," as Umberto Eco wrote in the last line of the *Name of the Rose*.[113] "There stands the pristine rose, and we hold only the naked name." What remains for teachers of history is that which stands before us. We bear the legacy of the past embedded in our discipline and in the institutions in which we work. In this sense, not only does history repeat itself, but so too do historians. The fact that each generation, as Lynn Hunt argues in the quote that started this chapter, asks its own questions of history keeps the discipline flexible and relevant. The nature of that relevance continues to be debated, and will likely always be debated. But it is clear that notions of personal fulfillment and civic duty remain constants. During the height of the Big Bang emphasis on "history in the service of patriotism," the National Education Report (1916) declared that history was indeed important for "good citizenship" but also for "the present life interests" of students.[114] Amid sharp cuts to the humanities in recent years, Charles A. Zappia, a dean at San Diego Mesa community college, argued that history has greater public utility than ever in helping create "a social good that benefits all."[115]

And if history appears to be "contested" nowadays, it is important to understand that this has always been true. Even in the halcyon days of "objective scientific" history transported from the lecture halls of German schools, with Ranke and Hegel providing the models of grand meaningful narrative, the role of the past in understanding the present was never entirely clear. In his *Lectures on the Philosophy of World History* (1837), Hegel himself wrote that:

> ... rulers, statesmen, nation, are often advised to learn the lesson of historical experience ... but what experience and history teach is this: that peoples and governments never have learned anything from history, or acted on principles deduced from it. Each age and each notion finds itself involved in such peculiar circumstances, in such peculiar circumstances, in such a unique situation condition, that it can and must make decisions with reference to itself alone.

---

112 Louis Menand, *The Marketplace of Ideas*, pp. 80, 81.
113 These are the final lines of Umberto Eco's *The Name of the Rose* (New York: Harvest Books, 1983), p. 502.
114 Novick, *Noble Dream* p. 188.
115 Bonnie G. Smith, Gender and practices of scientific history, p. 1150.

Hegel called this "pragmatical" history.[116] The modern historian will recognize Hegel's statement as a warning about extrapolating the present too narrowly from the past and the need for close attention to historical context.

Meanwhile, the "dead language and ancient people" curriculum of the early universities may be gone, but the basic pedagogical goal that lay behind it – "to better understand the human experience" – remains a fundamental part of teaching history. The approach is now ironically most evident in those multicultural, noncanonical, non-Western courses that were so virulently condemned by the guardians of the Western tradition. Historians of these "alternate" fields, as noted in Chapter 1, often appeal to students with insufficient backgrounds by finding common or even uncommon features of the human experience to provide a basic point of entry for study. Indeed, the coincidence makes a greater impression on students when familiarity or strangeness, two sides of the same coin, can be found in a place, time, and historical context that students know little about.

And as the university changes, many of the basic challenges of teaching history remain the same. Most fundamentally, professors are not universally masters of their own domains in the classroom. They are called upon to teach an array of courses that fit their institutions and curricula. I was required to teach Western Civilization when I arrived at Vanderbilt University and thus willy nilly inherited the cultural baggage that went with it.[117] I had no choice: the course was presented to me as "my tenure class" because it would prove that I could teach nonhistory majors, who were then required to take the class to fulfill university requirements. The test of my pedagogical skill thus involved mastering what Gilbert Allerdyce called a "wilted course," progressive scholars like Gary Nash and Peter Stearns condemned as a bastion of old-guard Western European chauvinism and conservative ideologues Lynn Chaney and the Bass brothers applauded as the salvation of American society.[118] I became the face of northwestern European hegemony even if my own face is decidedly Mediterranean, and my family, like so many from southern Italy (Puglia), fled the old country to escape poverty and prejudice and with a decided bias *against* the Anglo/Germanic world. Western Civilization was for me an egregious instance of Pirsig's motorcycle.

116 Georg W. F. Hegel, *Lectures on the Philosophy of World History*, edited by H. B. Nisbet (Cambridge: Cambridge University Press, 1975), p. 21.
117 William Caferro, Teaching Western Civilization. *Common Knowledge* 24:3, pp. 366–374.
118 Peter N. Stearns, World history: curriculum and controversy. *World History Connected*, 3:3 (2006).

My job was – and is – to make it work. I otherwise have no official opinion on the matter. I hope that students learn and think critically in that course, as I hope they do in my other courses.

The experience is widely shared by historians, who inherit courses that cover still broader arcs of time or do not correspond at all to their training. We embrace the challenge, even when it is not of our own making. And cultural wars aside, it is important to avoid equating too narrowly the backgrounds of an increasingly diverse professoriate with the subjects they study and teach. Direct correlation is too simplistic and runs the risk, however unintended, of affirming Bridenbaugh's offensive image of the "outer-directed" scholar. Increased diversity of the professoriate has added many overlooked and underrepresented fields. But subfields reflect in the first instance a scholar's intellectual interests, which derive from many factors that may correspond to or be at odds with a person's own background. Neslihan Senocak, a professor of medieval history at Columbia University, is a Muslim from Turkey but studies Christian confraternities owing to "the influence of her British professors" in graduate school.[119] My friends from working-class backgrounds explicitly avoid studying poverty and peasants because they do not wish to be reminded of such issues, even in historical distance. Other friends and colleagues of similar background openly embrace such topics. I remember once asking a colleague and friend at the University of Tulsa why he, "a big dumb Italian/Irish American from New Jersey," chose to study early modern China. I felt entitled to the outrageous question because of my own background and my colleague's wonderful sense of humor about himself. The question was also meant rhetorically. But he looked at me very seriously and replied, "You know, Bill, I wanted to get as far away from my past as possible." I understood viscerally. Education is transformative, especially for those whose backgrounds allow them to see clearly a very different alternative path. Indeed, studying Italy as an Italian-American was in my family a species of betrayal. They had abandoned the language (dialect), which marked them as outsiders, and identified strongly as Americans. Why go back and study northern Italy? Nevertheless, I found the materials for study of medieval economic and social history most compelling for Italy.

Finally, despite dire warnings about the current state of humanities, there is, as noted in Chapter 1, the very positive development of a discourse on pedagogy that treats teaching as a craft worthy of close scrutiny and mutual discussion. And amid the din of the "cultural wars," there grew university teaching centers, which have increased 300-fold in recent years

---

119 Interview with Neslahan Senocak.

and play a leading role in mentoring young faculty and communicating pedagogical approaches across disciplines at universities.[120] They take teaching as their "core value" and facilitate collaborations and exchanges that were unlikely to occur in earlier times (see Chapter 5).

The long view of teaching history reinforces, however, the importance of not adding too much order to the system, of avoiding a teleological grand narrative of progress that historians warn against in their own personal research. Contradictions proceed alongside continuities. Rather than a steadfast evolution of the methods of teaching history culminating in a technological revolution, there is the unsettling reality that teaching methods, even in the face of the internet, have not changed as much one would suppose. And any comprehensive and balanced assessment of effective teaching technique over time is limited by inadequate knowledge of how prepared teachers of yesteryear were with respect to their subject matter, how well they organized their classes, how enthusiastic they were for the materials they presented, how fair they were in assigning grades and, as Ernest Hartwell put it (see Chapter 1), how "familiar they were with the human experience."

What is undeniable, however, is that historians in all eras took creative, often quite different approaches to teaching. And as scientists have found with evolution in the natural world, older species often remain after the arrival of their replacement. The effective lecture class continued alongside the effective small seminar; textbook learning alongside careful reading of primary sources. Derek Bok, the former president of Harvard, speaks eloquently of a guiding ethos in his book *Beyond the Ivory Tower*.

> Every professor knows that much of the material conveyed in the classroom will soon be forgotten ... The willingness to continue teaching must always rest upon an act of faith that students will retain a useful conceptual framework, a helpful approach to the subject, a valuable method of analysis or some other intangible residue of lasting intellectual value.[121]

It should be added that the "intangible residue" involves instilling the desire and the tools in students to prepare them for life-long investigation on their own account. That is where true learning occurs.

---

120 Robert M. Diamond, The institutional change agency: the expanding role of academic support centers. In: *To Improve the Academy*, 23 (2005), edited by Sandra Chadwick-Blossey, pp. 24–37; Susan R. Singer, Learning and teaching centers: hubs of educational reform. *New Directions for Higher Education*, 119 (2002), pp. 59–64.
121 Derek Bok, *Beyond the Ivory Tower: Social Responsibilities of the Modern University* (Cambridge: Harvard University Press, 1984), p. 45.

3

"My Worst Day:" Classroom Management and Strategies for Success

"Do not teach *Praise of Folly* in your Renaissance Europe class," a colleague at Fairfield University warned me. "It is stilted, obscure and students do not get the humor. You will end up standing there scratching your head, talking to yourself." Since classrooms at Fairfield have elevated ledges at the front of them, I took the warning very seriously. It is one thing to look bad, but entirely another to do so standing on a platform.

Source: Donna Barstow cartoons

Teaching History, First Edition. William Caferro.
© 2020 John Wiley & Sons, Inc. Published 2020 by John Wiley & Sons, Inc.

I did not, however, listen to the advice. I saw a challenge and opportunity. I had never read *Praise of Folly* and wanted to use teaching it as an excuse to learn it well. In addition, I thought then – as I still do today – that educated people interested in the Renaissance and Reformation Europe (the title of my course then) should know this influential work by an important historical figure.

My colleague was right. The book fell flat or, more precisely, my teaching of it did. The students did not get the abstruse classical references, which challenge even a seasoned classicist. The humor shifts, and it is not always clear whether Folly is the proponent of satire or the object of it. My students in any case did not get the humor, shifting or otherwise. Indeed, humor from learned books does not as a rule transfer easily to university class discussions. The classroom is a formal setting that demands controlled and serious behavior from students, who often act quite differently outside of it. The more precise term is perhaps repression. That emotion makes it difficult to get them to laugh along with the authors they read, but renders almost everything else in the classroom funny.

But students can and do appreciate humor, especially satirical humor, if it is presented properly – indeed, if it is presented in the manner that Erasmus intended. The Dutchman's humor was not the problem with my class, nor were his classical references. The problem was the set-up of the reading assignment. With little time to prepare, I had hardly read my own assignment and did not introduce the book before the discussion and thus provided no context for understanding it. I failed, in fact, to do the very things that Professor Lieber at Columbia University was doing in his history classes at the turn of the twentieth century (see Chapter 2). The only intelligent thing I did was to require them to bring the text to class, which allowed us to go through specific lines together, highlighting the ambiguity of Folly and the basic nature of Erasmus's views.

The experience of humiliation is a familiar one. Jane Landers, who teaches Latin American history at Vanderbilt, tells a story of a friend at another university who posted a note on the cork board above his desk that read "next session, try to recapture the class." The Japanese novelist Natsume Soseki, himself a former teacher, portrays his main character Kenzo, a university professor, in his autobiographical *Grass on the Wayside* as a "pathetic figure standing at the podium," whose students would "look up and stare intently at his face" and "then solemnly write down all the half-baked comments." "He felt he was letting them down badly."[1]

---

1 Natsume Soseki, *Grass on the Wayside*, translated by Edwin McClellan (Ann Arbor: University of Michigan Press, 1969), p. 81.

We can all relate. Teachers at all levels have bad classes and there is no sure way to avoid them. Stephen Brookfield in *Becoming a Critically Reflective Teacher* explains well the nature of the challenge when he calls the classroom a "whirlpool of contradictory cross-currents."[2] What passes for common sense does not always work best. And what works for one teacher does not necessarily work for another. Paul Freedman, a medievalist at Yale University, notes that what worked for him at one stage of his career did not necessarily work at another stage.[3]

The successful teacher is a pragmatist focused on getting results (see Chapter 1). The sociologist Daniel F. Chambliss speaks of "the mundanity" of excellence. He argues that repeated "banal practices" lead to a few good encounters that positively shape a student's experience.[4] The road to success is not so narrow. And teachers must remember that there is a strong social dimension to learning that transcends the individual pedagogical virtù of an instructor. Friendships with peers and the overall environment at an institution affect learning, as well as the relation between students and their families at home. Professors rarely create motivation *ex nihilo*, but more often seek to direct it or not to lose it. Conversely, the instructor is not steadfastly responsible for circumstances that impede learning.

The discussion below focuses on five teaching activities: time management, classroom management/assignments, class discussions, lecturing, and grading. The list is not comprehensive, but represents basic tasks for all instructors of history. A discussion of technology, which now affects all aspects of teaching, is reserved for the next chapter.

Time Management

Time management is not only a problem for professors, but an eternal human struggle. "If you don't know where you are going," said the famous philosopher Yogi Berra, "you'll end up somewhere else." For starting teachers, the task is daunting because they rarely see distinctly the path forward and are confronted with unfamiliar challenges. The contrast to the final stages of dissertation writing is stark. The former involves an inevitable degree of social isolation and managing one's time in a void.

---

2 Stephen Brookfield, *Becoming a Critically Reflective Teacher* (San Francisco: Jossey-Bass, 1995), p. 5.
3 Interview with Paul Freedman.
4 Daniel F. Chambliss, Doing what works: on the mundanity of excellence in teaching. In: *The Social Worlds of Higher Education*, edited by Bernice Pescosolido and Ronald Aminzade (Thousand Oaks: Pine Forge Press, 1999), pp. 424–433.

The first teaching job replaces isolation with circuit overload. Rather than find distractions, one must avoid them. The task is greater now owing to the endless stream of emails from students, colleagues, and university administrators that frustrate attempts to separate work time from personal time.

The experience of the starting teacher is seared into my mind because of the numerous times I have played the role. My first "start" in college was as an adjunct at Fairfield University; my second start, with a different set of classes, was at the University of Tulsa; my third start was at Vanderbilt University, again with new classes. I had previously taught at two secondary schools over three years, as both a math and history teacher. I say without hesitation that the transition was never the same and it was never easy. There was always the fear of the unknown, lack of familiarity with the routine of the institution, colleagues and the courses I was required to teach. And creating new courses is always a formidable task.

Nevertheless, for all the rhetoric about the difficulties of the transition to teaching, it is important for instructors to avoid the urge to see themselves as martyrs. As David D. Perlmutter has argued in an essay for the *Chronicle for Higher Education*, it is "an exercise in self-indulgence."[5] And the ugly truth is that the challenges do not go away. Even for senior faculty at the same institution, there are committees to deal with, essays to referee for scholarly journals, books to evaluate for scholarly presses, tenure files to write and a whole range of activities that take time away from teaching. This is a basic difference between teaching at a university and in secondary school, and the reason why, despite an enduring sympathy, I do not support colleagues at major liberal arts institutions who publish little but champion themselves as teachers first. Juggling the two obligations is the essence of the job. Those who do not want to do this should set aside their egos and work in secondary school, where one has a still greater impact on young minds. They will likely find that they neither have additional time nor receive greater appreciation.

It is notable that university professors who endorse teaching often do so in terms of research and writing. The British historian Geoffrey Elton in his *Practice of History* (1967) argued that scholarship, or "lotus eating" as he called it, is fundamentally connected to teaching because it makes scholars more aware of "audience" and the importance of clearly stating their arguments. Elton did not, however, ask the question from the other side: how does scholarship affect teaching? The proper answer is that scholarship makes us better teachers. Gilbert Highet in his well-known

---

5 David D. Perlmutter, Do you really not have the time? *Chronicle for Higher Education* (August 2008), pp. 2–3.

Art of Teaching states forcefully that "knowing a subject well" is the most important aspect of good pedagogy.[6] Putting together ideas and presenting them in creative and rigorous ways has a fundamental appeal to students. Many of us are in fact university professors because we encountered an instructor who impressed us with a deep understanding of a subject and the ability to raise questions we had not thought of. Judith Brown, former dean of Rice University and provost of Middlebury College, stresses in an essay in *The Chronicle of Higher Education* that the stereotypical opposition between the good teacher and the good scholar is a myth. In her experience, the best researchers were often among the best teachers.[7]

In terms of preparation for classes at the start of the semester, scholarship is nevertheless (see Chapter 1) an undeniable competitor for one's time. For the beginner, the competition comes just as the need to publish is the greatest. And in the Hobbesian state of nature that is the academy, teaching burdens vary significantly from institution to institution. John H. Ball, a historian at Hillsborough Community College in Tampa, Florida, teaches five classes per semester. Laura Hohman, a historian at Trivecca Nazarene University in Tennessee, teaches four classes each semester.[8] Professors at major research institutions usually have a two-class load per semester. Large schools often have large lecture classes; small schools often have more intimate seminar classes. Most colleges have a combination of the two.

It would be incorrect to treat the large and small classes as opposites. Some faculty find it easier to teach lecture classes that are not in their specialty because they are less likely to get bogged down in detail and more likely to approach the material like their students. Corey Tazzara at Scripps College in California teaches only small seminars, but notes that the format means that he must carefully read and reread all the texts he assigns to facilitate class discussion.[9] The University of California at Berkeley calculates that new faculty need about 36 hours a week to prepare for three courses or four hours of preparation per class hour.[10] Nate

---

6 Gilbert Highet, *The Art of Teaching* (New York: Alfred A. Knopf, 1950, reprint 1989), p. 12.
7 Stated in Claire Potter, On the nature of change in higher ed (part III): assessing the costs. *Chronicle of Higher Education* (November 19, 2011).
8 John H. Ball, Teaching at a community college: some personal observations. *Perspectives on History* (April 1 2010); www.historians.org/publications-and-directories/perspectives-on-history/april-2010/teaching-at-a-community-college-some-personal-observations; interview with Laura Hohman.
9 Interview with Cory Tazzara.
10 Office of Educational Development at the University of California. https://teaching.berkeley.edu/home and http://americanfacultyassociation.blogspot.com/2012/02/hours-for-teaching-and-preparation-rule.html

Kreuter in his essay "The math doesn't work" argues that there is in fact no faculty member, tenured or untenured, who actually works the standard 40-hour week. He uses 60 hours as the baseline for a 3/3 teaching load, but notes that for faculty with lesser teaching responsibilities, the number of hours does not change, only the allocation of them does. More time is spent on research during the semester, which is required of that type of job.[11]

The bottom line is that there is little time for preparing class (see Chapter 1). And it is worth adding that even if some professors had more time, they would likely not use it. Few enjoy the process. Robert Boice of the State University of New York at Stoney Brook makes an excellent case in *Advice to New Faculty* for "timely waiting," by which he means that first-time instructors should avoid "over-attachment and overreaction" in their preparation.[12] Boice gave his book the Latin subtitle *Nihil Nimus* or "nothing to excess" to emphasize the point. Failure for starting professors often comes from an inability to control one's emotions. "Quick starters" are optimistic and often have a sense of humor.[13] Self-irony makes labor of any kind easier and is crucial for longevity.

Optimism, humor, and emotional distance are all helpful. So too is personal self-confidence and the ability to avoid the innate desire to be loved. The latter is a problem particularly for graduate student TAs, who sometimes seek validation in their lonely pursuit of the PhD through close contact with students. Secondary school teachers receive some version from their supervisors of Machiavelli's "it is better to be feared than loved" and understand right away that authority is best projected by not catering to the masses. "One of the hardest things" for college teachers to learn, writes Stephen Brookfield, "is that the sincerity of their intentions does not guarantee the purity of their practice."[14] It is myth to believe that we will be perceived the way we wish, and emotional neediness is easily detected – and disliked – by intuitive students at all levels. Students respond to those instructors who implicitly put their needs first.

To better understand a teaching environment and audience, it is important to seek advice from colleagues and consult the syllabi of other professors in the department and speak with members of teaching

---

11 Nate Kreuter, The math doesn't work. *Inside Higher Education* (April 2013). www.insidehighered.com/advice/2013/04/22/essay-hours-faculty-members-work-each-day
12 Robert Boice, *Advice to New Faculty: Nihil Nimus* (San Francisco: Jossey-Bass, 2002), pp. 1–2.
13 Robert Boice, Quick starters: new faculty who succeed. *New Directions for Teaching and Learning* (Winter 1991), pp. 112–113.
14 Stephen Brookfield, *Becoming a Critically Reflective Teacher* (San Francisco: Jossey Bass, 1995).

centers. The culture of a department and institution plays a significant role in the way we teach (see Chapters 2, 5). The online Open Syllabus Project lists more than a million syllabi and even sorts them in rank order according to the most popular books used in classes (at present Strunk's *Elements of Style* and Plato's *Republic* are numbers 1 and 2).[15] It is a tacit experience of sharing, but a useful one, and participants are encouraged to add their own syllabi to the collection. Scholars of pedagogy also suggest that beginners read course catalogues for the description classes, talk frequently with colleagues to get a sense of the rhythms of daily class and the workings of their institutions and expectations of students.[16]

The most difficult decision is what *not* to include in a course.[17] Advocates of the "backward design" model of course preparation, which has received a great deal of attention, suggest using a small set of "lynchpin ideas" that highlight broad issues of "enduring value." Grant Wiggins and Jay McTighe, prominent proponents of backward design, warn of the "twin sins" of "standard" course design: creating assignments "simply for the sake of engagement" and trying to cover "all the material."[18] Backward design helps shift the focus from the professor and the performative aspects of teaching to the student and the reception of knowledge. Rather than provide a cursory overview of vast amounts of information, the professors go into depth on selected issues and have students undertake "critical analysis" of material that mirrors what professional historians actually do. The approach has been strongly advocated for secondary school by pioneers such as Bruce VanSledright, Larry Cuban and others who stress the importance of "student-centered" learning as an antidote to the long tradition of the teacher-centered/dry recitation of facts approach.[19]

The aim is to get students to "think historically" and actively interrogate the past. The advice must, however, be followed with care. Wiggins and McTighe cite as an example of a "lynchpin idea" the Magna Carta, the great medieval English document from 1215, imposed by barons on King John I.

---

15 http://opensyllabusproject.org
16 Greg Conderman, Ten tips on course preparation. In: *Field Guide for Teaching in a New Century: Ideas from Fellow Travelers*, edited by J. H. Shin, D. Pike, D. Rome, and B. A. Pescosolido (Thousand Oaks: Pine Forge Press, 1999), p. 31.
17 Barbara Gross Davis, *Tools for Teaching* (San Francisco: Jossey-Bass, 1993), p. 3.
18 Grant P. Wiggins and Jay McTighe, *Understanding by Design* (Alexandria: Association for Supervision and Curriculum Development, 1998), pp. 13–33.
19 Larry Cuban, *How Teachers Taught: Constancy and Change in American Classrooms, 1890–1990*, 2nd edn (New York: Teachers College Press, 1993); Bruce A. VanSledright, What does it mean to think historically... and how do you teach it? *Social Education*, 68:3, pp. 230–233 and *Assessing Historical Thinking and Understanding: Innovative Designs for New Standards* (New York: Routledge, 2013).

They assert that it provides the "model of written law" that would later become the "cornerstone of modern democratic societies."[20] Few medievalists would unfortunately agree with the statement, which ignores another basic historical principle – context. Magna Carta is a distinctly medieval document, which called for the English king to respect his traditional feudal obligations to his nobility. It had important implications for the future but most immediately, it exposes a fundamental difference between modern notions of democracy and "liberty" and medieval notions of feudal obligations. To use Magna Carta as "a lynchpin idea" for discussion of modern democracy is more worrisome still because it reeks of the old Anglo-Saxon/northern European chauvinism that was common in history courses at nineteenth-century American universities (see Chapter 2), where English values stood as the precursor of American values. It also contradicts Sam Wineburg's notion that "historical thinking" is "unnatural" and cannot be easily translated to modern-day students, as well as the dictates of the National Council for History Education (NCHE), which call for instilling in students "historical empathy" to replace "present-mindedness," which the Council condemned as "downright dangerous" intellectually.[21]

The vast majority of events that occurred in the distant past do not have a precise analogue in the present, which is itself an important species of historical thinking. Understanding that distinction is a valuable lynchpin idea. Backward design is nevertheless a crucial development, but it must be deployed in a manner that takes into consideration the various challenges posed by study of the distant and unfamiliar past.

Classroom Management and Assignments

Regardless of the amount of time devoted to preparation and teaching strategies, success depends greatly on basic classroom management. There are good and bad habits. Secondary school teachers are specifically instructed on this; university professors are not. My supervisor in high school told me to move about the classroom when I taught, to make sure to seat the students where I wanted, to casually invade their space as

20 Grant Wiggins and Jay McTighe, *Understanding by Design*, p. 15.
21 This is stated in the section "History's habits of mind," which calls empathy a "core principal of historical study": www.nche.net. Stephane Levesque cites historical empathy as one of his five essential goals at the heart of historical education. Stephane Levesque, *Thinking Historically: Educating Students for the Twenty-First Century* (Toronto: University of Toronto Press, 2008), pp. 37–38.

I spoke, especially that of the ne'er-do-wells in order to keep their attention. She told me to inspect the room before class began, to arrange the tables as I wanted (if they were not rooted to the floor), keep it tidy, pick up trash, and repeat this after the students left, so that the next group would be arranged as I wanted. The point was to pay attention to detail! She told me to raise my hand if students called out answers and that the students would then imitate me and be more orderly. I scoffed inwardly, but it worked.

Colleges, with their more transcendent intellectual missions, provide uneven guidance in this respect, and the guidance is not necessarily well received. Professors often immure themselves behind front desks and lecterns, look down as they speak or pace back and forth; few fuss with the arrangement of the room or pick up after the students. But this is not so problematic in the college setting because bad behavior by students is not a present threat. College students signal their lack of interest by not listening. And if the student does not wish to listen, it is of course their own responsibility. University education is expensive and some students seem determined to get less than their money's worth.

Nevertheless, it is vital that we be heard. A constant for classroom management at any level is that the instructor be organized and make clear the expectations for students with respect to grading, attendance, assignments, and the general goals of the course.[22] Making expectations explicit, however articulated, conveys the sense of joint enterprise. And as in secondary school, few students have problems with rules as long as they know what they are. Stating them at the outset, both in written form and by verbal reminder, has the benefit of dispassionate dissemination and the undivided student attention. It lessens the likelihood that the instructor will in fact have to employ punitive measures, since rules work best when they do not have to be enforced. For me, handing back assignments quickly (within a week) is an essential tool of control. It emphasizes the sense of mutual responsibility, enhances the likelihood that feedback will make its mark, and, more generally, shows that what the professor demands from the student, she/he demands of herself/himself. I steadfastly avoid self-reflective comments regarding any personal teaching challenges in the class, since students rightfully do not care. It is about them.

Nevertheless, human relations are inherently unstable and professors have decidedly different personalities. One should not dismiss out of hand the effectiveness of the "fly by the seat of their pants" professors,

---

22 The Center for Innovative Teaching and Learning at Indiana University offers videos on classroom management. https://citl.indiana.edu/teaching-resources/teaching-strategies/classroom-management/

with their brilliant asides, distracted mien and loose course structure.[23] Ken Bain in his book on excellent teachers speaks of "remarkable" instructors whose methods "offend disciplinary purists."[24] In *The Skillful Teacher: On Technique, Trust, and Responsiveness in the Classroom* (2015), Stephen Brookfield points out that many of the basic prescriptive assumptions about university teaching can in fact be problematic. "Progressive" professors who seek to deconstruct their authority and act more informally "in order to overcome the insecurity of students" may in fact appear falsely modest and inadvertently create mistrust from students who prefer overt teacherly authority that makes it more clear to them where they stand. Additionally, Brookfield argues that while it may seem self-evident that more experienced teachers invariably have the best instincts, they may be more closed off to students and lack the immediacy of the younger teachers, who connect better on account of their age. A critical if seemingly banal observation is that instructors are at their best when they are comfortable with their own personas, which implicitly translates itself to the course, giving it a basic authenticity. All teachers, to paraphrase Ken Bain, must "find their own genius" and build upon it. This is, however, not an easy task. The notion of "know thyself" has befuddled philosophers since antiquity.

Inasmuch as students project themselves into a class via the assignments, a basic question is what does a good assignment look like? The strategies, as noted in Chapter 1, vary significantly from professor to professor and course to course. A constant is that students dislike, and rightfully so, classes for which there are few assignments, especially when they come at the end of the semester. The practice limits the drudgery of grading for the professor, but students need to know how they are doing along the way. Experts on pedagogy agree that the most effective strategy is one that evaluates a variety of student skills.[25] Professors should establish explicit learning guidelines and course objectives and create assignments that assess these desired outcomes.[26]

---

23 Ken Bain, *What the Best College Teachers Do* (Cambridge: Harvard University Press, 2004), p. 8.

24 Ken Bain, *What the Best College Teachers Do*, p. 21.

25 Mirilla Svinicki and Wilbert J. McKeachie, *McKeachie's Teaching Tips* (Belmont: Wadsworth, 2006), pp. 72–82: Tom Angelo and Pat Cross, *Classroom Assessment Technique: A Handbook for College Teachers* (San Francisco: Jossey-Bass, 1993); Laurie Richlin, *Blueprint for Learning: Constructing College Courses to Facilitate, Assess and Document Learning.* (Sterling: Stylus Publishing, 2006); Bruce A. VanSledright, *Assessing Historical Thinking and Understanding: Innovative Designs for New Standards* (New York: Routledge, 2013).

26 Jay McTighe and Grant Wiggins, Understanding by Design® framework. www.ascd.org/ASCD/pdf/siteASCD/publications/UbD_WhitePaper0312.pdf

Short "response" papers may be used to summarize and critique specific sources. Oral presentation can be used to examine a student's ability to process information and articulate it clearly to others. Longer papers can be employed to assess students' skill in presenting a sustained critical interpretation of a broader historical idea or set of sources. Midterms and finals can assess the mastery of basic course material and performance in a pressured, limited-time environment. Quizzes can keep students up to date with the readings and save them from their basic impulse toward inertia.[27] The prominent scholars of pedagogy Thomas Angelo and Pat Cross speak of a "feedback loop" that involves an ongoing give-and-take in which teachers "open the loop" by assigning various tasks and complete it by giving feedback for improvement along the way. [28]

There has been a great deal of recent discussion about how to construct effective assignments to foster active learning and "historical thinking" in students. Advocates of so-called inquiry-based methods suggest that teachers assign "meaningful historical problems" that raise questions about historical narratives and problematize events.[29] The National Education Association (NEA) offers an "authentic assessment toolbox" aimed at implementing a curriculum that measures student achievement in direct ways, through a series of tasks that encourage students not only to learn information but to "gain experience" in a way of thinking and undertake collaborative work.[30] In a similar vein, historians employ project-based learning (PBL), which emphasizes self-directed student learning and begins with a central question or task that students narrow down and dissect.[31] Stéphane Lévesque in *Thinking Historically: Educating Students for the Twenty-First Century* isolates five essential questions "framed to uncover a certain procedural concepts," including continuity and change in the past and how we may understand predecessors who had different moral ideals.[32] The Center for Teaching at Drexel College in Philadelphia suggests 4–7 well-crafted learning outcomes that focus on broad skills.[33]

27 John C. Bean, *Engaging Ideas: The Professor's Guide to Integrating Writing, Critical Thinking, and Active Learning in the Classroom* (San Francisco: Jossey-Bass, 2011).
28 Tom Angelo and Pat Cross, *Classroom Assessment Technique*, pp. 6, 9, 31.
29 Robert B. Bain, They thought the world was flat? Applying the principles of how people learn in teaching high school history. In: *How Students Learn: History, Mathematics, and Science in the Classroom* (Washington, DC: National Academies Press, 2005), p. 184.
30 www.nea.org/tools/lessons/57730.htm
31 Web pages for Sam Houston State www.shsu.edu/centers/project-based-learning/higher-education.html and Boston University www.bu.edu/ctl/guides/project-based-learning/
32 Stéphane Lévesque, *Thinking Historically: Educating Students for the Twenty-First Century* (Toronto: University of Toronto Press, 2008), p. 37.
33 https://drexel.edu/provost/assessment/outcomes/developing-course/

The goal is always to get students to engage actively and critically with source material. It is surprising, however, the degree of disagreement there has been over the issue. Barret Havens in an essay for *The Chronicle of Higher Education* (2013) was taken aback at the tenor of discussion regarding student assessments, which, he notes, are linked in the first instance to accreditation of universities which comes from outside and above and is perceived by some as invasive.[34] Robert T. Dillon, a long-time professor at the College of Charleston, complained of being pressured by his university to place mandated learning outcomes on his syllabus and his forceful disagreement led to charges of insubordination.[35] Erik Gilbert, a professor of history at Arkansas State University, who helped craft the learning assessments for his school, noted ironically that he did not consider these in choosing a college for his own kids.[36]

Writing

Nevertheless, the importance of active engagement and critical thinking is manifest and hardly controversial. For teachers of history, two of the most basic assignments are writing and reading – fundamental skills of historians that are transferable to students' daily and professional lives. Most students, given the current state of public education in America, come to college with limited practice in either, especially in writing. Professors at junior colleges spend a large portion of their time on basic remedial work relating to sentence structure. But even students from more fortunate educational backgrounds, including private school, often do not know the difference between a verb, noun, and adjective. For this reason, the Vanderbilt History Department requires as its basic objective to have students write as often as possible. My colleague Michael Bess requires students in his popular World War II class to write a thematic paper on the readings every day. Paul Freedman at Yale uses short frequent writing assignments for freshman classes at Yale University, but longer ones for history majors. Jennifer Spock at Eastern Tennessee finds that longer papers do not fit the type of classes and students she teaches – the latter often dividing their time between school and full-time jobs. Instructors find shorter assignments more practical and effective and easier to critique.

---

34 Barret Havens, Give assessment a fighting chance (November 4, 2013) www.chronicle.com/article/give-assessment-a-fighting/142773?cid=rclink

35 https://drexel.edu/provost/assessment/outcomes/developing-course/

36 Erik Gilbert, Does assessment make colleges better? Who knows? *Chronicle of Higher Education* (August 14 2015) www.chronicle.com/article/does-assessment-make-colleges/232371?cid=rclink

It is here, as we shall discuss in greater detail in the next chapter, that technology has had an important impact. Blogging, Wikipedia entries and other online activities provide professors with additional ways of engaging students in writing. They allow instructors to increase the amount of writing students do, and also alter student perception of audience – a *key* component of any form of writing (see Chapter 4). At the same time, however, the internet has diminished attention spans, and frequent writing in the form of text messaging and emails to friends often occurs at the expense of good grammar and sustained argumentation. In addition, students may now "google" facts that they do not know rather than memorize them. This affects historical writing which, however we present it, requires some basic mastery of facts.

It is not surprising, then, that students generally prefer shorter essays to longer ones. In an article in the *Washington Post* (2010), based on interviews with college freshmen, Jay Mathews concluded that many students have in fact never done a long paper in high school.[37] I came to a similar conclusion during a recent stint as director of undergraduate studies. I took an informal and unscientific poll of student opinion and found a dislike for papers longer than five pages, owing to unfamiliarity and fear of being unable to sustain an argument. John Warner, an adjunct writing instructor at the College of Charleston and a columnist for the *Chicago Tribune*, complained that students arrive at college unable to write because of "a near-exclusive diet" of "five-paragraph essays," aimed at "parroting existing information" and preparing for standardized tests.[38] Warner called for an outright ban on them from secondary school curricula, arguing that they render students unable to undertake sustained critical analyses.

Like many colleagues, I use longer papers alongside shorter response papers aimed at assessing different skills. They work well together in that the shorter papers encourage close reading by students of a specific reading, which helps facilitate longer more critical papers related to several readings. The short papers also keep students on track and facilitate classroom discussion. I usually pair short response papers with brief oral presentations on the same material. The fear of speaking publicly serves,

---

37 Jay Mathews, Long papers in high school? Many college freshmen say they never had to do one. *Washington Post* (July 15, 2010) www.washingtonpost.com/wp-dyn/content/article/2010/07/13/AR2010071304642.html?noredirect=on
38 John Warner, I cannot prepare students to write their (history, philosophy, sociology, poly sci., etc...) papers. *Inside Higher Ed* (December 15, 2015) www.insidehighered.com/blogs/just-visiting/i-cannot-prepare-students-write-their-history-philosophy-sociology-poly-sci-etc, and *Why They Can't Write: Killing the Five Paragraph Essay and Other Necessities* (Baltimore: Johns Hopkins University Press, 2018).

at least for me, to focus my attention and force me to know the subject matter well. My former colleague at University of Tulsa, Jeff Hockett, calls these "peak performances," assignments that students pay the greatest attention to. Once one has spoken on a topic, they are often in a better position to write, particularly because they often receive feedback from the other students. It also simulates what historians do: write up results, present them before an audience (conference), listen to comments, respond and revise. When the audience misses the point, it should be taken as a sign to make the argument clearer.

Historians agree that the greatest challenge with respect to writing assignments is the research paper. It is our peculiar burden, as it stands at the core of our craft. But research papers are exacting, and expose most clearly Warner's complaint. Moreover, the requirements vary from subfield to subfield. It is particularly difficult for students to do research for topics on the distant past or those unrelated to America or England. The research paper uncovers in this respect the hidden aspect of the historian's task: the importance of knowing the language(s) of the subject one studies. It is, as noted in Chapter 1, enthusiasm for this that often draws a scholar to her/his subfield in the first place. But it is here that our roles as teachers and scholars often diverge most strongly. The medievalist Samantha Kelly of Rutgers University notes that the problem for her field is not only a lack of student background in language, but that the sources themselves, when rendered into English, are often "too technical" or "too poorly translated" to be of much use.[39] Indeed, medieval Latin texts, especially those translated in the early twentieth century and most readily available on the internet, are often converted into a species of Victorian English, which lends an air of importance to the "dead" language but is historically inaccurate and, worse, distances students still further from the past. There are no "thees" and "thys" in Latin.

It may well be the case that the only true research college student paper is that which deals with modern America and England. But the process, no matter what the field, requires a mixture of both intellectual rigor and flexibility. Close reading of sources allows students to develop questions but the question will inevitably change with greater engagement in the sources. It is the Heisenberg uncertainty principle in action. Students are not accustomed to this and it may be here that Sam Wineburg's notion of history as an "unnatural act" strikes a particular chord.

The web page for the history department of Carleton College provides a lucid account of the basic steps for writing research papers. It suggests that students begin with a pertinent question based on a first look at

---

39 Interview with Samantha Kelly.

primary and secondary sources. Students must read materials critically and consider the purpose and intended audience of the primary documents. They must then sketch out an outline of major ideas and be prepared to go through numerous drafts.[40] The history department of Hamilton College requires that students do careful "historical analysis" in their papers, which requires that they "dig beneath the surface, to see relationships or distinctions that are not immediately obvious." With a nod to David Letterman, the web page for the department lists the "top ten" problems with paper writing. Prominent among them is "cheap anachronistic moralizing," which professors will readily agree is a very common problem. Thinking historically does not mean neatly aligning the past with the present.

At Vanderbilt, we devote a separate class to the research paper. We allow five weeks for reading on a topic, then require the students to develop a preliminary research question along with a preliminary bibliography. We then ask the students to do outlines and rough drafts that we critique directly with them and pass among the students for peer review.

The internet continues to revolutionize the availability of primary source material. The Archaeology of Reading in Early Modern Europe digital project begun in 2014 by the libraries at Johns Hopkins, Princeton and University College in London has made available searchable scans of old printed books with the marginal notes of readers. It allows students and scholars to examine the manner in which texts were received and understood by what was highlighted and annotated by the reader. Stanford University's website "Beyond the Bubble," created in conjunction with the Library of Congress World Digital Library, offers a wide range of texts and visual images. One can find the original version of the Articles of Confederation, Napoleon's Description of Egypt, sixteenth-century anatomical texts, and maps from different eras. The web page also has helpful suggestions for teachers, including potential questions and annotated student responses, as well as videos that give additional insight into assessments and ideas for teaching.[41]

Reading

Historians face similar challenges with respect to reading assignments. Unlike the sciences, history requires weekly readings rather than daily problem sets. The task is therefore more easily put off by students, which

---

40 https://apps.carleton.edu/curricular/history/resources/study/writing/
41 https://sheg.stanford.edu/history-assessments

makes the choice of assignments and oversight of them all the more important. In my generation, I am sad to say, historians around the water cooler would often boast of the length of their reading assignments to demonstrate their pedagogical rigor and toughness. Recent studies suggest, however, that there is a law of diminishing return. In an article in *USA Today* (December 2013), an undergraduate at Princeton University complained of "a culture of skimming" reading assignments at the school. This was not on account of laziness, but because "too many pages were assigned each night." Skimming engendered "insincerity," such that students learned how to *appear* prepared and speak in learned generalities, making, as Socrates complained in antiquity, the lesser argument appear the better.[42]

Insincerity is the last thing a teacher wants to impart to students. Finding the right number of pages is indeed a problem. The guidelines I inherited – "one hundred pages a week" – always perplexed me. The size of a reading assignment depends on the type of material, the level of the course, the particular subfield and, more elementally, the availability (and cost) of the texts themselves. One must always keep at the front of their minds the learning objectives of a course. Unfamiliar primary source material is more difficult to read than secondary source material and requires more careful attention. The length of an assignment must also correspond to how much a teacher feels that students can rightly absorb and how much they themselves are prepared to cover carefully in class. Anthony Molho of Brown University looked back to his first teaching experience in middle school as critical in convincing him of the importance of moving slowly and carefully through books. Students absorbed more. As a college professor, Molho found success devoting significant amounts of time to "complicated" works like those of Fernand Braudel and Marc Bloch. Samuel K. Cohn, a professor of medieval history at University of Glasgow in Scotland, prefers shorter, focused texts. He has found that big books like Jacob Burckhardt's *Civilization of the Renaissance in Italy* do not work for him in class. Students get lost in complex narrative and are unable to extract the larger ideas.[43]

Caroline Bynum puts it best when she advises that weekly readings should be chosen not only to provide background and basic information for students, but also "to challenge their assumptions." "Anything that bores the professor will probably bore the students too."[44] Here again, active engagement and critical thinking are key. Shorter "more

---

42 Dan Reimold, Princeton student: stop skimming through reading assignments. *USA Today* (December 20, 2013).
43 Interview with Samuel K. Cohn.
44 Caroline Bynum, Teaching about objects. *Common Knowledge* 23:1 (2017), p. 67.

manageable" pieces are not the obvious remedy. The landscape of college history teaching is in fact flooded with course readers that offer brief predigested snippets of primary source material, intended to get "at the heart" of a source and spare students the tedious whole. They are popular in some large lecture classes. I avoid them, even in my Western Civilization class, which is the largest class I teach. I prefer that students read a substantial piece of a single author's work. I find that the most interesting and rewarding material is often not the "core" snippet of an argument, but the periphery and "nonessential material," which better helps give the context of the argument and often leads to still more productive discussions. But, again, the assignment must fit the class and the institution. Jennifer Spock at Eastern Kentucky University finds that her students, with full-time jobs, respond well to short primary source reading, which she puts on the screen in front of the class and goes through with them sentence by sentence. She requires the students to take notes on the reading and show them to her in class.[45]

The nature of college reading assignments has recently become, like so much else in the academy, the subject of a spirited, politicized debate. In an essay entitled "Getting students to do the reading" posted on the website of the National Education Association, Linda Nilson, director of the Office of Teaching Effectiveness at Clemson University, advised faculty "to accommodate reality" and appeal to students on their own level by assigning "readings with graphics and pictures that reinforce the text and to pare down the required pages to the essentials."[46] The opinion elicited a strong response from Carlin Romano, a professor at Ursinus College and the University of Pennsylvania, who denounced Nilson's approach as part of an ongoing overall dumbing down of the academy. He called it "extreme academe" and saw it as part of a "destructive cultural trend" that contradicts the basic mission of teachers.[47]

The balance is a delicate one. Professors must keep in mind pragmatic goals, while at the same time engaging their students. The misconception is that professors can clearly apprehend the social and intellectual world of their students and know their likes and dislikes. This involves the implicit false premise that students indeed represent a single category. Here Caroline Bynum's advice to use one's own sensibilities as a basic measure is most pertinent. We are most enthusiastic when we teach what we enjoy, which is a crucial and difficult to quantify aspect of successful teaching.

---

45 Interview with Jennifer Spock.
46 www.nea.org/home/34689.htm
47 Carlin Romano, Will the book survive generation text? *Chronicle of Higher Education* (29 August 2010).

There is perhaps no reading assignment that is more controversial than the textbook. It recalls the "tweedy" history professor of yesteryear and stokes unfortunate generational divides among present teachers. Woodrow Wilson, like many of his contemporaries in the early twentieth century, stressed "textbook drill" as the most basic teaching tool (see Chapter 2).[48] The cognitive behaviorist Sam Wineberg condemned textbooks as presenting little more than a "referential illusion" about history. They give students the impression that the reality of past events is fixed, which is precisely the opposite of the critical thinking needed for study of the subject. Michael Conway in a recent essay in *The Atlantic* similarly derides the "set narrative" of the textbook. He calls it a "single standardized chronicle of several hundred pages" of little real worth.[49] James Loewen has gone still further in his popular book *Lies My Teacher Told Me*, denouncing textbooks (notably those used in secondary school American History classes) as propagating "willful falsehoods" and "startling errors of omission and distortion."[50]

Textbooks nevertheless remain widely used, and may indeed always be part of university teaching. Wilbert McKeachie in his *Teaching Tips* describes textbooks as having had "a greater influence on what students learn than any other teaching tool."[51] The guidelines of the American Historical Association published in 1997 stress the "vital role" played by them in history education, from elementary school through college survey courses. The report states that a good textbook offers "a distillation of available knowledge" and helps with the "development of appropriate historical habits of the mind beyond memorization." Indeed, the award given by the American Historical Association for the "most outstanding contribution to the teaching and learning of history in any field for public or educational purpose" is named after James Harvey Robinson, author of the standard textbook for Western Civilization, *An Introduction to the History of Western Europe*, published in 1902.

Thus, referential illusion or not, textbooks cannot be dismissed out of hand. And a close look at Robinson's famous tome shows that the genre was not so simplistic at the beginning of the twentieth century as we may reflexively suppose. Robinson stated a strong skepticism about organizing history around dates and "a simple set of facts." He expressed a distaste for the traditional focus on political history and advocated a "more

---

48 Herbert Baxter Adams, *The Study of History in American Colleges and Universities* (Washington, DC: US Government Printing Office, 1887), pp. 214–215.
49 Michael Conway, The problem with history classes. *The Atlantic* (March 2015), p. 12.
50 James W. Loewen, *Lies My Teacher Told Me* (New York: Touchstone, 2007), p. 7.
51 Wilbert McKeachie, *Tips for Teaching: A Guidebook for the Beginning College Teacher* (Lexington: D.C. Heath, 1986).

thematic" approach.[52] The title page of the book forcefully reminds us of this. It quotes the French historian Fustel de Coulanges (d. 1894): "History is no easy science, its subject; human society, is infinitely complex." The same statement is heard in one form or another in present-day classrooms. Robinson argued for a "living history" – a past that continues into the present and answers the question "How did we get this way?" The goal is not dissimilar to the "lynchpin ideas" advocated by Grant Wiggins and Jay McTighe, and much of the recent literature that connects the past to the present!

A comparison of current university textbooks with those of yesteryear is beyond the scope of this book but it is worth pointing out that the genre has not changed as much over the years as publishers would like us to believe. Jackson Spielvogel's *Western Civilization*, the most popular in its field, follows Robinson in stating explicitly its intention to go "beyond" the current focus on political history (haven't we already?). But where Robinson describes his methodology in full sentences, Spielvogel relies more on partial phrases, outlines, and charts. The narrative and historical analyses are reduced to digestible morsels, set off in colorful boxes that catch the eye. Each chapter starts with a box labeled "critical thinking" and "connections to today" – making explicit basic pedagogical principles. The chapters end with glossaries of key terms.

The book fits Linda Nilson's guidelines for visual appeal and paring down of written material to its essentials. But it raises more questions than it answers, including whether "critical thinking" can in fact be reduced to boxes. Meanwhile, the reduction of the narrative to short bursts of simplified information sends a subliminal message that stands in sharp contrast to the sustained argumentation that college professors seek. This is not to say that the genre has not made strides. Women played no role in Robinson's textbook in 1902, but figure prominently in Spielvogel's book. Robinson focused largely on England, Germany and France, while Spielvogel and other Western Civilization books now include coverage of Islam, Byzantium, and Russia. The old narrative of European New World exploration has become relativized in terms of other peoples.

A practical problem, however, is that in making textbooks more visually appealing, publishers have increased the price of them exponentially. Over the last decade alone, prices have risen a full 82%. And while publishers make it possible now "to rent" a textbook, the economics are still sinister. Poorer students in open enrollment schools are less capable of

---

52 James Harvey Robinson, *An Introduction to the History of Western Europe* (Library of Alexandria, 1902), pp. iii–iv.

affording them. Several community colleges in Virginia, including Lord Fairfax College, Tidewater College and Northern Virginia College, have experimented with open source materials on the web for classes in American history. The Hewlitt Foundation and other charitable organizations have invested in online open educational resources (OER) to make available textbooks and a wide range of books for free. The OER Commons has material ranging in level from elementary school to college, with links to specific subject areas, educational groups, and hubs for further material.[53]

Nevertheless, each year a representative of a major book company knocks on my door to sell me a textbook. I always listen and ask questions because they are doing their jobs and deserve respect. I tried to phase the textbook out of my Western Civilization class but the students objected. They felt more secure with a textbook. They were accustomed to it from high school, which was usually the last time they took such a survey. The dangers of "referential illusion" are mitigated by the fact that professors in college invariably also assign primary source readings for class discussion, and place emphasis on explication of those in their assessments of students. The textbook as sole source is most common in secondary schools, and I must confess that when I taught in that venue, my supervisors in fact encouraged that practice.

It is nevertheless important to remember – and in fairness to the authors of them – that there are good textbooks books out there. Jennifer Spock enjoys using Bentley and Zeigler's *Traditions and Encounters* in her World History class because it focuses on interactions among cultures, which students enjoy and stimulates conversation. She has found the detailed maps particularly helpful. And inasmuch as her scholarly training was medieval Russia, the textbook helped her assemble the course which involved material she was not familiar with.[54] Many of us do the same, especially at the start of our careers, the textbook being as useful to the professor as to the student. I read Warren Hollister's *Medieval Europe* before first teaching that subject. And though it focused on England, kings and queens – subjects that do not interest me – I really liked the book, especially because the author had a sense of humor.

It is also important to understand that such texts do indeed represent referential illusions and that it is our responsibility to make students aware of this. As Sam Wineberg sagely notes in his critique of Howard Zinn's widely used and controversial *People's History of the United States*, whatever the point of view of the author, the text must not be viewed as

---

53 www.oercommons.org
54 Interview with Jennifer Spock.

a "single answer" representing the "real" set of facts. History is always about "multiple causalities." Indeed, James Loewen's critique of secondary schools textbooks, for all its virtues, posits an "alternate" version of American History that the author presents as a greater truth ("The Truth about Thanksgiving," according to one chapter). A sociologist by training, Loewen depicts historical facts as settled and subject to the choice of an author. But historians do not treat history this way, and, as Sam Wineberg and Jose Antonio Bowen argue in their recent books, critical and skeptical reading of "facts" is especially necessary in the current day where more historical information resides on a smartphone than in a university library.[55]

Class Discussion

In his famous autobiographical sketch (*The Education of Henry Adams*), Henry Adams pointed to class discussion as the most vexing aspect of his troubled academic career. It is, he wrote, difficult to get students to talk and the instructor is left with the responsibility of "devising schemes to find out what they are thinking and to risk criticism from their fellows." A "large body of students stifles the student."[56]

Adams highlights key issues. Class discussions are wild cards for teachers. They are unpredictable and affected by factors outside the instructor's direct control. They depend on whether students do the reading, whether they are shy or self-confident, whether the class is large or small; the type of room, the gender and racial balance and even the time of day or week that the class meets. Peter Frederick in his aptly entitled essay "The dreaded discussion" lists among his greatest pedagogical fears "the terror of silence."[57] And since no discussion is the same as another, the search for a standard model is elusive. "In a seminar format," Richard Davis of Bard College argues, "I am not sovereign lord of the classroom. Students respond to the readings, to me, and to each other, with enthusiasm or disinterest. That becomes part of the classroom dynamic."[58]

---

55 Sam Wineberg, *Why Learn History (When It's Already on Your Phone)?* (Chicago: Chicago University Press, 2018); Jose Antonio Bowen, *Teaching Naked: How Moving Technology Out of Your College Classroom Will Improve Student Learning* (San Francisco: Jossey-Bass, 2012).

56 Henry Adams, *The Education of Henry Adams* (Boston: Houghton Mifflin, 1918), pp. 301–302.

57 Peter Frederick, The dreaded discussion: ten ways to start in teaching and the case method. In: *Teaching and the Case Method*, edited by Louis B. Barnes, C. Roland Christensen and Abby J. Hansen (Boston: Harvard Business School Press, 1994), pp. 90–91.

58 Interview with Richard Davis.

C. Roland Christensen, a professor at Harvard Business School, calls the discussion section "the art of managing spontaneity."[59] Professors must know their material well, keep the big picture in mind and try not to do too much. Mary Harvey Doyno at Sacramento State University rereads her texts carefully before her class on early Christianity to "have the words and sentences in the forefront" of her mind to facilitate greater flexibility in the classroom.[60] Caroline Bynum seeks to ensure "that everyone is included" and to establish "robust conceptual categories to guide discussion in the following weeks."[61] Bynum believes that there should "be a road map charting where the instructor hopes the exploration will go yet leaving space for the unexpected to emerge."[62]

A common element is creating an environment of trust and support. Bynum arranges her students initially in groups so that they get to know each other and make connections across grade levels, majors, and preexisting friendships. This helps engender a "congenial competitive spirit."[63] Derek Bruff, director of the Teaching Center at Vanderbilt University, suggests strategies that encourage students to respond directly to each other rather than to the teacher, since students are otherwise not naturally inclined to listen to each other.[64] Jennifer Spock uses impromptu role playing in class, which she admits is a concession to the reality that her students lack knowledge of the subject they study when they enter her classes. For discussion of the Silk Road, she divides the class into groups representing the major regions involved. The students discuss what they have to sell and what they want to buy. Although some students are reluctant to do this, Spock notes, "they never forget what they learned that day."[65]

Whatever the strategy, the goal is to get the students to think historically, create a critical learning environment and generate discussion as much as possible from within rather than from the outside, by professorial decree. For me, the first step, fashioned after my unfortunate experience with *Praise of Folly*, is to frame the reading and pose basic questions about it in advance. In classes involving lecture and discussion, I gear my lecture around the reading. In seminar classes, I pose questions about next week's reading at the end of class, after discussion of the current

---

59 C. R. Christensen et al., eds, *Education for Judgment: The Artistry of Discussion Leadership* (Boston: Harvard Business School, 1991).
60 Mary Harvey Doyno, Where in the text. *Common Knowledge* 23:1 (2017), pp. 5–7.
61 Caroline Walker Bynum, Where in the Text? Symposium: In the Humanities Classroom. *Common Knowledge* 23:1 (2017), p. 68.
62 Walker Bynum, Where in the Text? Symposium: In the Humanities Classroom. p. 67–68.
63 Frederick, The dreaded discussion, p. 91.
64 Interview with Derek Bruff.
65 Interviews with Derek Bruff, Jennifer Spock.

reading. In both cases, however, I supply specific questions, usually three, about issues students should contemplate as they read. I pose the questions with the presumption that the material is new to them and that this will help provide an entrée into the unfamiliar. I remember my own experience as an undergraduate math major reading Petrarch's *My Secret* in a class on Renaissance Europe. The dialogue between Petrarch and Augustine is fictive but I did not know that. So I diligently recorded in my notes the points made by both, favoring in general the statements of Augustine, who seemed the more compelling figure to me. When we arrived in class, the professor asked only about Petrarch and told us that Augustine was clearly "an invented foil" who bore no resemblance to the real person. I had no idea, and wondered why he did not say something about that earlier.

The advance questions form the basis of class discussion, but only the basis. I prepare others, indeed more than I ever actually use. Some colleagues ask students to prepare questions themselves and circulate them prior to discussion via the internet. Others have students write questions down on a piece of paper when they enter class and then choose from that list. Each has the advantage of fostering discussion from within. My concern with questions on a sheet of paper at the start of class is that students sometimes ask questions that are not answerable or that require strictly factual answers that go beyond the course. Skilled teachers can of course restate and reformulate these questions. I find that using my own questions as an entrée often encourages them to ask their own. I restate and reformulate these when necessary, and also have developed a tendency to repeat student answers to project them to the others to make sure they are listening, or to restate and tweak answers to nudge the conversation in a perhaps more productive direction.

Sam Wineberg and the Stanford History Education Group provide excellent advice about the types of questions to pose to students. They suggest focusing on interpretive issues and avoiding simple "yes/no" or "leading" questions. Wineberg employs categories such as "sourcing," questions about the circumstances of the authorship and creation of a document; "contextualizing," situating the source in terms of other themes and events; and "close reading," looking closely at the language of the document, which may involve accounting for the silences.[66] The web pages of numerous teaching centers suggest using a version of "Bloom's Taxonomy," formulated in the 1950s, which arranges strategies into a

---

66 Sam Wineburg, Thinking like a historian. *Teaching with Primary Sources Quarterly*, 3:1, Winter 2010. www.loc.gov/teachers/tps/quarterly/historical_thinking/pdf/historical_thinking.pdf; https://teachingcommons.stanford.edu/resources/teaching/student-teacher-communication/designing-effective-discussion-questions

pyramid, at the bottom of which is information recall and at the top is evaluation and analysis.[67] The online Padeia Active Teaching Seminar advocates a Socratic text-based method that includes also "maieutic" questions that seek to get students to relate class issues to their own lives.[68] The Derek Bok Center of Teaching at Harvard offers a "tip sheet" of typologies that suggests diverse questions: general "open-ended questions" to facilitate entry into a subject by establishing basic information, "diagnostic questions" to get at interpretation, "challenge questions" that pit answers against each other, "priority questions" that ask students to establish a hierarchy of importance, and "extension questions" which can lead to still broader considerations.[69]

The common element is the need for a realistic and considered strategy to elicit active engagement of students with course materials. And it should be added that what professors ultimately choose to do should also correspond to what they feel most comfortable doing and include always showing respect and support for the students. I am myself not agile off-script like many of my colleagues and so I manage the spontaneity of discussion in a more controlled and rehearsed manner. My first question usually strikes at a basic theme, with a bit of provocation. If the text is Augustine's *Confessions* I ask the standard: "Why *did* Augustine and his friends steal the pears from that tree and why did it bother him so much?" The question is informational and allows a rehashing of the text, which gets the class talking about specifics. The question is also interpretive, touching an important overall theme of the work: why does evil exist in the world? I find it useful, like other professors, to pose "extension questions," to ask a student who has answered to clarify his/her point further.

Drawing on my experience as a high school math teacher, I try to keep my own formulations brief to facilitate rather than dominate student discussion. Economy of expression worked best when I taught math, so I am inclined to do so as a college history teacher. I speak as little as possible at the start of class. No matter how insightful I believe my comments may be, a long prologue in my experience encourages students to revert to a passive role. I remember the advice I got my very first day as

---

67 B. S. Bloom, *Taxonomy of Educational Objectives: The Classification of Educational Goals: Handbook I, Cognitive Domain* (New York: McKay, 1969); L. W. Anderson, D. R. Krathwohl, and B. S Bloom, *A Taxonomy for Learning, Teaching, and Assessing: A Revision of Bloom's Taxonomy of Educational Objectives.* (New York: Longman, 2001).
68 www.paideia.org
69 https://bokcenter.harvard.edu/leading-discussions; https://docs.google.com/document/d/1DtjufyIZQcpavotn68O7rmXmd48lUNcK30FuLW0MXA4/edit; see also S. A. Ambrose, M. W. Bridges, M. DiPietro, M. C. Lovett, and M. K. Norman, *How Learning Works: Seven Research-based Principles for Smart Teaching* (Chicago: John Wiley & Sons, 2010).

a teacher: "It is about them" and discussions give students an opportunity to shine intellectually. Since I was too reticent as a student to participate in discussion sections, I have the habit of looking at those who are not speaking. It often causes them to look up at me. If I see a small movement, I sometimes politely ask the student to share an opinion. The result is usually a reluctant but outstanding answer. I try to engage the shy students as early as possible in a discussion before inertia sets in and the social hierarchy of the class becomes too fixed. I often subtly address students outside class, just before or just after, and ask how they are and how things are going. Sometimes all I get is a pained smile, but I want them to know that I know who they are. For all my own reticence as a student, it meant something to me when the teacher knew me. If I disconcert those who wish to remain anonymous, well, maybe that is not necessarily a bad thing.

Nevertheless, it is an ongoing process of understanding nuances such as when to interrupt the flow of a discussion, how to encourage but also criticize, and also how much we can cover. Here again, an atmosphere of respect and empathy is crucial. I come to discussion class with a list of major points I intend, no matter what, to get across. I use 5–10 minutes toward the end to add these points to our discussion if we have not covered them and then pose questions for the next reading. I keep in mind that the kinetic, "all hands in the air" discussion – for some the transcendent pedagogical ideal – is not as effective as some teachers, particularly beginners, believe. There are conversations and there are conversations. Anna Neumann, the former president of the Association for the Study of Higher Education, makes plain that "it is not enough for faculty development experts – or higher education researchers – to say that students are engaged in class. What they are engaged with – and how they engage it – matters still more."[70] To avoid being swept up in the moment, I refer back to my notes, at the ideas I wish to get to, and again, I look at those students who are not speaking. What are they hearing or not hearing? I try always to bring us back to the text and have students read pertinent parts aloud. Mary Harvey Doyno has one student read a passage slowly, while another puts it into the everyday vernacular. This keeps her students engaged and allows her to move from general questions to more specific ones and vice versa.

This type of heuristic circle is useful and helps bridge the gap between the students and the "unnatural" historical sources they read. Again, basic classroom management is essential. It helps to learn students'

---

70 Anna Neumann, Staking a claim on learning: what we should know about learning in higher education and why. *Review of Higher Education*, 37:2 (Winter 2014), pp. 263.

names as soon as possible, and have the students learn each other's names and address each other by them. The geography of the classroom matters. It is difficult to conduct any real interchange of ideas in a lecture classroom designed for many students. I prefer a seminar table or a room in which students can see each other without obstruction. But here again, prescriptive assumptions can miss the point. Stephen Brookfield points out that while "progressive educators" prefer to have students sit in a circle to create a species of "pedagogical democracy," he cites research that shows that the "amiable circle" is ambiguous. For the confident student, it is both congenial and liberating but for shy students and those of different racial and ethnic backgrounds, it can be a painful experience, making them feeling as if their privacy is being violated.[71] Proponents of dividing class into small groups point to the utility of engaging students on their own terms, directly with each other, encouraging them both to participate and listen. The professor serves as "guide by the side" and research by scholars such as Carol Tomlinson and Rick Wormeli indicates that the practice promotes "differentiated learning" – faculty can better accommodate differing skill and readiness levels, interests and learning profiles of the students.[72]

There are still more innovative and effective strategies. Professors and universities are experimenting more with place-based learning, connecting the classroom to local communities. Students engage in real-world projects. At Antoich College in Keene, New Hampshire, faculty and students work together with the Horatio Colony Nature Preserve on issues of ecological stewardship and sustainability.[73] Meanwhile, Harvard Business School pioneered a more traditional "case study" form of intellectual engagement. Students are asked to respond to a specific source, a vignette, often a legal one, and interrogate it jointly together, without preliminary information. Students "learn to the question."[74] My colleague Ari Bryen uses translations of short papyrus inscriptions from Ancient Rome (usually no more than 15–30 lines) and asks the students first to tell what they think about the document. Once the questions begin to

---

71 https://sta.uwi.edu/cetl/wshops_events/events/openlectures/documents/UWIGLO
penLecture2009-SBrookfield.pdf
72 Carol A. Tomlinson, This issue: differentiated instruction. *Theory Into Practice*, 44:3 (June 2010), pp. 183–184; Rick Wormeli, *Differentiation: From Planning to Practice, Grades 6-12* (Portsmouth: Stenhouse Publishers, 2007); Grant P. Wiggins, *Educative Assessment: Designing Assessments to Inform and Improve Student Performance* (San Francisco: Jossey-Bass, 1998).
73 www.antioch.edu/new-england/resources/centers-institutes/center-place-based-education/
74 John Boehrer and Marty Linsky, Teaching with cases: learning to question. *New Directions for Teaching and Learning*, 42 (Summer 1990), pp. 42–43.

blend into a narrative, he intervenes to suggest a counternarrative, and discusses the larger implications of supporting one version or the other.

Lecturing

No topic has elicited stronger opinion in recent years than lecturing. Much of the pedagogical literature casts the practice in a negative light, as a "passive" form of intellectual engagement as opposed to "active learning" and "critical thinking" that professors now encourage.[75] Lectures constitute "dry transfers of information" that render student minds "inert."[76]

Lecturing is nevertheless part of a long and distinguished tradition that goes back to the Middle Ages. Gilbert Highet attributes it in the first instance to a scarcity of books, which required medieval students to write down every word, to "create a notebook of facts."[77] Woodrow Wilson, our erstwhile spokesman for dated pedagogy, lauded the lecture as essential to history. He wrote that it "opens out the horizon necessary for a real understanding of the special tracts of history which are being traversed." Wilson's ideal lecturer highlighted the "most memorable characteristics" of a period and explained the "philosophical connections" among facts.[78] In other words, the lecture was *not* a dry transfer of facts but an interpretation of the *meaning* of the facts. It served as an entrée into critical thinking rather than an inert competitor.

In any case, disdain for lecturing is unhelpful and disingenuous. Historians often teach lecture classes because they are required to do so. Indeed, it is important that historians know how to lecture well in order to present their scholarly work at professional conferences and to get jobs at on-campus interviews. Those who teach at community college or at large schools with large numbers of students and little infrastructure to accommodate them often have little option but to lecture. And, ironically, the same internet technology that facilitates "flipping classes" has produced the Massive On-Line Courses (MOOCS) that have made the "old-fashioned" lecture format available to world-wide audiences (see Chapter four). Thus, just as critics reject lecturing, universities and

---

75 Kenneth A. Eble, *The Craft of Teaching* (San Francisco: Jossey-Bass, 1988), pp. 68–82.
76 Lendol Calder, Uncoverage: toward a signature pedagogy. *Journal of American History*, 92:4 (2006), p. 1364.
77 Gilbert Highet, *The Art of Teaching*, pp. 93–94.
78 Herbert Baxter Adams, *The Study of History in American Colleges and Universities*, p. 222.

companies like Coursera, which manage MOOCS, have validated it in a global context and make significant amounts of money from it.

Ken Bain strikes the right note when he points out in his study of "excellent" teachers that rigid oppositions shed little light on good pedagogy.[79] And it remains the fact that writing and giving an effective lecture require a great deal of work. It involves first conceptualizing a topic, then writing it out, editing, rehearsing and finally delivering the lecture before a live audience. The last part is in some ways the most problematic. It involves an emotional state that cannot be predicted in advance. Patricia Nelson Limerick put it well when she called lecturing "an act for which providence did not design humans."[80]

The lecture is performative, difficult and time-consuming and some professors find that easier than others. This simple fact may be why it evokes such visceral disagreement. Nevertheless, in the hands of a gifted thinker/speaker, the lecture may indeed serve, as Woodrow Wilson argued, as a stimulating entrée into history and inspire students to the very type of active engagement that critics seek. At its most basic level, the lecture provides a model of intellectual engagement and excitement for students, which Ken Bain sees as essential to great teaching.[81] Students see, perhaps most clearly, the intersection between their professors and the subject matter they teach.

For this reason, I do not shy away from providing information in my lectures that goes beyond the books and beyond the level of my students. I apply the same principles to the lecture as my scholarly writing. I begin with a basic question, contextualize it, juxtapose alternate interpretations and raise larger questions. My hope is that, if stated clearly and simply, the lecture will convey "critical thinking" and provide an impetus for students to seek a similar level of active intellectual engagement or shoot still higher. I seek to tap into the energy and passion that made me become a professional historian. Anthony Molho was inspired to become an historian in large part because of the "rhetorical gems" that were the lectures of his professors Jack Greene and Marvin Becker. He remembers that the men were "full of energy and inspiration" and their observations were "laced with brilliant insights and occasional bits of humor." The lectures were not just occasions for imparting information to students, but opportunities to in fact "challenge students'assumptions and suggest new interpretations."[82]

---

79 Ken Bain, *What Great Teachers Do*, pp. 98–99.
80 Patricia Limerick, Aloof professors and shy students. In: *On Teaching*, edited by Mary Ann Shea, vol. 1 (Boulder: University of Colorado, 1987), p. 4.
81 Ken Bain, *What Great Teachers Do*, pp. 13–18.
82 Interview with Anthony Molho.

The fact that Anthony Molho remembers lectures from 40 years earlier says a great deal about the genre. As a student, I found heartfelt inspiration from the lectures of Jaroslav Pelikan. I was in awe of his learning and his ability to articulate clearly, directly and elegantly the most abstruse aspects of medieval theology, which he had mastered in all the original languages. I wanted to be like him, to be part of his club. And during my time as undergraduate director for the history department at Vanderbilt, I found that a consistent and surprising complaint among students was about those history classes in which the professor did *not* give lectures. Students complained about insufficient background for historical information and implicitly, I believe, conveyed the feeling that with discussion alone, class was too informal and insufficiently organized. The lecture gave the implicit message that the professor was, to use the language of today, "all-in."

Gilbert Highet in his popular (albeit dated) *The Art of Teaching* compared the university lecturer to a species of opera singer. He gave practical advice such as varying one's voice, "changing tempo" and "employing pauses."[83] He warned against reading lectures word for word, which is tedious for everyone involved. Highet's advice is helpful but one must also take care to distinguish between speaking well and speaking insightfully. The two are not always the same; the best is achieving both. It does not necessarily follow, for instance, that a nervous lecturer is an ineffective one. Nervousness may evoke a degree of discomfort from the audience, but it does not erase the message if it is well thought out. Indeed, it may be argued that the sight of an otherwise reticent professor working through her/his nervousness, emboldened to move forward by love of the subject material, is a compelling one. It humanizes the professor and underscores a still more important implicit message that intellectual engagement is transformative.

I say this perhaps as personal justification, because I am myself a nervous lecturer. But because of that trait, I rehearse my lectures over and over and focus on the quality of the material as a way out of my own cycle of fear and self-doubt. I practice my lecture in my office before class. I pace with the lights off and speak the words out loud. I put notes in the margin that Highet would have approved of – "look up," "slow down" and "try to look like you are actually enjoying this." My personal discomfort standing in front of the room has not been a hindrance insofar as it has made me work harder at preparation and at letting my knowledge, as it were, carry me rather than my personality. But for that same reason lecturing exhausts me, I do not like it, and Professor Pelikan remains my transcendent model.

---

83 Highet, *The Art of Teaching*, pp. 95, 96, 99, 103, 105.

Grading

Grading has been placed at the end of the chapter but if the "Art and Craft of Teaching" class at Vanderbilt is any indication, it belongs first. No task is more difficult for professors at the start of their careers, and consideration of it returns our discussion to where we began, with time management. Grading is both time-consuming and innervating. Natsume Soseki provides a stark image in *Grass on the Wayside* of his main character Kenzo sitting before a pile on papers. "As he read each one he would stop now and then to draw in red ink ... occasionally he would rest his eyes and gaze disconsolately at the seemingly undiminished pile."[84]

The feeling is widely shared. And the burden of grading is not fairly distributed. Professors at small elite schools mark less than those at large nonelite institutions. Meanwhile, the quality of student work also affects grading. Good work takes less time to mark than bad work. And in addition to time-consuming, grading can be outright perilous. Instructors endure baleful stares and angry emails from disappointed students who believe that they deserved better. Recent studies connect low student grades with bad teaching evaluations. And bad reviews can now be available for all to see, courtesy of the world-wide web and forums like ratemyprofessor.com.

There is in short a lot at stake. Peter Elbow speaks of "competing loyalties in the classroom." Professors want their students to be allies in a mutual commitment to knowledge, but they must also serve as "bouncers" with respect to grading.[85] And grading is not an exact science. The range of available marks is inadequate to the task. In an influential study, Ohmer Milton and John Edgerly (1976) argued that teachers use "unidimensional symbols" to report what are in essence "multidimensional phenomena."[86] And the university grading system, which began in the eighteenth century, has not advanced much over the years. At Yale University in those days, students were evaluated according to four Latin categories, ranging from *optime* (excellent) to *pejores* (bad). The Latin is gone but the basic divisions remain. In 1884, Mount Holyoke initiated a system based on A, B, C, and D, adding an F (for failing) in 1898.[87] At the University of Tulsa, the available grades were precisely the same: A, B, C, D, and F. At Vanderbilt,

---

84 Natsume Soseki, *Grass on the Wayside*, pp. 153–154.
85 Peter Elbow, *Embracing Contraries* (Oxford: Oxford University Press, 1987), p. 459.
86 Ohmer Milton and John W. Edgerly, The testing and grading of students. *Change Magazine* (1976), p. 44.
87 James O. Hammons and Janice Barnsley, Everything you need to know about developing a grading plan for your course (well, almost). *Journal on Excellence in College Teaching*, 3 (1993), p. 52.

and most other schools, grades are nuanced to include minuses and pluses. But as professors know all too well, the B range is particularly elastic and students with often very different skills end up in that category. And a grade below B+ is likely to set off complaints.

Ahmed Afzaal of Concordia College in a recent essay in *The Chronicle of Higher Education* (2012) warns of an "unhealthy attitude" among students about grades that derives from 12 years of "socialization" with parents and high school teachers who create the assumption that effort alone is enough to earn high scores.[88] These students, Afzaal writes, do their assignment with the belief that they begin with a perfect score that is reduced by the professor. Grade inflation has become a widespread means of stifling discontent and calming the masses. Students who receive high grades usually complain less. Thus, it is an ugly professional reality that some professors take the path of least resistance to obscure pedagogical flaws in their classes, which might otherwise be exposed.

Nevertheless, grading is difficult for young professors and especially so, as the graduate students in the Vanderbilt seminar note, for TAs, who do not set down the guidelines but nevertheless must enforce them. Grade scales vary from class to class and professor to professor. A key first step, no matter what the circumstance or level of experience, is, as noted throughout this chapter, to make assessment criteria as clear and transparent as possible to students. The rules should be stated clearly on the syllabus, and communicated verbally along the way. For a TA, it is useful to meet with the professor to discuss common strategy (this is of course the responsibility of the faculty) and after an assignment to exchange papers and discuss mutual impressions. In my experience, this often diverges and professors have stored up experience of institutional practice and student expectations that should be shared.

Barbara Gross Davis in *Tools for Teaching* provides excellent advice that instructors should grade holistically, to provide diverse assignments to get at a variety of skills (as noted above) and to grade something early in the semester to give students a clear sense of the scale.[89] Many professors give a grade for class participation and weight assignments differently to account for improvement over time. For Western Civilization, where I have TAs who run sections, I make the class participation component worth more than in my other classes to underscore the importance of the section and help the TAs.

---

88 Ahmed Afzaal, Grading and its discontents. *Chronicle of Higher Education* (July 2012). www.chronicle.com/article/GradingIts-Discontents/132789

89 Barbara Gross Davis, *Tools for Teaching*, 2nd edn (San Francisco: Jossey-Bass, 2009) p. 233; Carolyn S. Lieberg, *Teaching Your First College Class: A Practical Guide for New Faculty and Graduate Student Instructors* (Sterling: Stylus Publishing, 2018), p. 163.

The Center for Teaching at Stanford recommends that instructors be in "a good frame of mind" when marking and find a comfortable environment to do so. It gives additional advice to read several papers and exams and make a first round of comments in pencil before putting on final grades. The Center for Teaching at Vanderbilt recommends that professors look through papers and exams twice and with an interval in between, to ensure fairness and equity.[90]

Such advice is easier to follow for professors with smaller classes. But I have tried throughout my career to adhere to the suggestions, even when teaching large introductory courses (without TAs), with the proviso that I begin reading papers and exams the same day I receive them. This builds momentum for me. Looking at even a few papers and exams is helpful in creating basic parameters and, more selfishly, in creating reassurance that I will indeed get the task done expeditiously. I read a set number each day, regardless of my schedule (nowadays five or six; in my adjuncting days ten to eleven). If I read too many consecutively, I am inclined to take out my frustrations on the last set. Conversely, I may have too high a standard for the first ones I grade. I put my comments in pencil. When I am done with all of them, I scan them again and adjust the grades as I feel it is needed, and put the final mark in ink.

Experience in this aspect of teaching matters. Lynn F. Jacobs and Jeremy S. Hyman argue in an essay in the *US News and World Report* that it in fact becomes "relatively easy" for seasoned teachers to distinguish between good papers and exams and bad ones.[91] There is much truth in the statement. For me, a "comfortable environment" to mark is a public place, usually a coffee house, with other people around, where ambient noise strangely helps me focus. I often grade in the later afternoon. This is not because my mood is better then; in fact, I am most able to think clearly first thing in the morning. But I reserve that time for academic writing. In the later afternoon, I am often already tired, less resistant to grading and less inclined to talk to myself when I see the same mistake over and over again. I hand back assignments within a week, a habit that was ingrained in me during my time as a secondary school teacher as a fundamental part of the learning process and projection of teacherly authority.

What precisely constitutes *effective* grading is the subject of a great deal of literature. Harry Edmund Shaw in "Responding to student essays" recommends that professors offer specific remedies for correcting

---

90 Gilbert Highet, *The Art of Teaching*, p. 123.
91 Lynn F. Jacobs and Jeremy S. Hyman, 10 Things you didn't know about college grading. *US News and World Report* (November 2009). www.usnews.com/education/blogs/professors-guide/2009/11/04/10-things-you-didnt-know-about-college-grading

writing rather than placing imprecise terms such as "awkward" or "unclear," which have little utility, in the margins.[92] Some colleagues complain that flagging grammatical mistakes is often too much of a burden and takes away from consideration of critical thinking and thematic structure. I find it hard to separate the components, as clarity of expression for me is connected to content and the type of critical thinking that lies at the core of the historical process. But professors must, by necessity, focus on a limited set of issues and flagging a few well-chosen examples will likely have a greater impact on students than a sea of red ink. A former colleague would write "see me" on the most problematic papers, and then tell the student directly the problems with the paper to augment the comments and make sure they are heard. I have adopted this myself but do not restrict it to the worst papers, but include also those with problems that I think are typical and fixable through discussion. I often have students read problematic passages and ideas to me out loud from their papers. It is critical to be kind and supportive, since this is not easy for them, but the routine has produced reasonable success. Other colleagues report good results from marking papers online, using Track Changes and then discussing electronically issues of content and form, then offering rewrites.

Tests represent their own pedagogical challenge, and are especially controversial in recent years in secondary school, where "teaching to the standardized test" has become an unfortunate measure of teacher quality. Experts like Bruce VanSledright challenge whether such "high stakes testing" encourages the type of historical thinking that history teachers seek to elicit.[93] Nevertheless, most of my colleagues agree that college students perform better on tests than they do on papers, perhaps because of their prior education. Students who cannot express themselves well or present sustained arguments in papers nevertheless can demonstrate critical thinking on essay questions and identifications.

The results, of course, depend on the nature of the exam. Blue books, a vestige of the Big Bang days, dating from the 1920s, remain a fixture in college history classes. Their origins (and why they are blue) are the subject of debate, but they were intended in the first instance to replace oral recitation.[94] Jennifer Courtney has argued that blue books get at the

---

92 Harry Edmund Shaw, Responding to student essays. In: *Teaching Prose: A Guide for Writing Instructors*, edited by Fredric V. Bogel and Katherine K. Gottschalk (New York: Norton, 1984), pp. 116, 129, 133, 137.

93 Bruce VanSledright, *Assessing Historical Thinking*, pp. 114–115.

94 Jennifer Courtney, How blue book exams get at the heart of assessment. *Classical Conversations* (2014); Barbara Gross Davis, *Tools for Teaching*, pp. 239–299. www. classicalconversations.com/article/how-blue-book-exams-get-heart-assessment

"heart of assessment," but this depends, of course, on the nature of the blue book exam. The University of Washington Center for Teaching and Learning suggests the assignment of essays which, although "subjective," nevertheless require sophisticated historical thinking and written expression.[95] I assign both essays and identifications.

I create the essays from themes based on primary document reading and class discussion of them. The identifications are historical events, which students must identify and give an "historical significance," which in turn involves linking the events to the overall historical themes of the course. I do not try to deceive but use rather straightforward identifications, aimed at finding out how well they understand history and have processed the material. To this end, I give the essays out a week in advance: a list of four from which I pick two for the exam. We have a review session beyond the regular class time, usually a weekend day, and I bring pizza. I smile inwardly to myself, feeling that I have perpetrated a clever trick, adding an extra session of intense student-led discussion. I encourage the students to form study groups, which promotes not only critical thinking but also camaraderie against a common foe (me and my exam)!

I unabashedly admit that I believe in the efficacy of the timed test. They do indeed exert pressure, sometimes painful, on students. But learning how to manage that pressure is, in my opinion, a useful skill for students to bring with them into the "real" world. David Perry, a historian at Dominican University, has, however, decided to abandon the blue book on the grounds that it is unfair to students with disabilities and forces them to expose their condition and potentially subjects them to bias.[96] He prefers take-home exams.[97] There is little empirical research on the benefits of one versus the other. Researchers at Virginia Tech in 2003 concluded that those who took in-class tests appear to have retained information longer.[98] But whether this is the ultimate goal of an exam is debatable.

Finally, it needs to be said, as the graduate students in our seminar at Vanderbilt duly note, that tough grading can result in negative student

---

95 www.washington.edu/teaching/teaching-resources/preparing-to-teach/constructing-tests/. See also Barbara Gross Davis, *Tools for Teaching*, p. 272.

96 David Perry, Why I'm saying goodbye to in-class tests. https://chroniclevitae.com/news/1410-why-i-m-saying-goodbye-to-in-class-tests

97 Michele Willins, Do in-class exams make students study harder? *The Atlantic* (December 21, 2015). www.theatlantic.com/education/archive/2015/12/take-home-vs-in-class-exams-mixed-feelings-and-results-on-campus/421281/

98 W. J. Haynie, III, Effects of take-home tests and study questions on retention learning in technology education. *Journal of Technology Education*, 14 (Spring 2003). https://scholar.lib.vt.edu/ejournals/JTE/v14n2/haynie.html

evaluations. Graduate school is, whatever else may be said about it, an often lonely, isolating experience. Positive feedback is all the more important and, unfortunately, the TA is often the one who stands at the forefront of criticism, even if the faculty sets the rules. In a witty essay in *Slate* magazine (24 April 2014), Rebecca Schuman stated bluntly that the student evaluative process is so grade driven that it is worthless. Positive evaluations necessitate "sucking up to the students," which led Schuman to conclude that "asking students to evaluate their professors anonymously is basically like Trader Joe's soliciting Yelp reviews from a shoplifter."[99]

Philip Stark, chairman of the statistics department at the University of California at Berkeley, points out a more basic problem: sample sizes are insufficient to make the results meaningful. And response rates have gone down in recent years with the advent of online evaluations. Undergrads, overloaded with email and social media messages, often ignore the review prompt, leaving teachers at the mercy of those most strongly motivated to respond: students who loved the class and students who hated it.[100] Neither set of reviews offers much in the way of useful advice. And the effectiveness of evaluations depends on the nature of the questions posed, and these are not always thought out carefully. Recent studies show biases based on race, gender, age, ethnicity, and class size. Women face "contradictory and unrealistic expectations" that are different from those of their male counterparts.[101] The alternative, peer review by faculty, has received attention lately, but it also has flaws. Faculty supervisors are sometimes committed to their own methods and not always tolerant of others. They are not trained in the job of teaching evaluation and thus bias will not necessarily be eliminated.[102] There is, however problematic, logic to having the consumer of the product have an opinion about it. A recent suggestion is creating a

---

99 Rebecca Schuman, Needs improvement: student evaluations of professors aren't just biased and absurd – they don't even work. *Slate* (April 2014). www.slate.com/articles/life/education/2014/04/student_evaluations_of_college_professors_are_biased_and_worthless.html

100 Philip Stark, An evaluation of course evaluations. *ScienceOpen* (2014). www.stat.berkeley.edu/~stark/Preprints/evaluations14.pdf. See also Terry Doyle, Evaluating teacher effectiveness. In: *Research Summary of the Center for Teaching, Learning and Faculty Development* (Ferris State University, 2004) and Kathleen S. Crittenden, James L. Norr, and Robert K. LeBailly, Size of university classes and student evaluation of teaching. *Journal of Higher Education* 46:4 (1975), pp. 461–470.

101 Colleen Flaherty, Bias against female instructors. *Inside Higher Education* (January 11, 2016). www.insidehighered.com/news/2016/01/11/new-analysis-offers-more-evidence-against-student-evaluations-teachin

102 Daniel J. Bernstein, Peer review and evaluation of the intellectual work of teaching. *Change* (March/April 2008).

portfolio that involves, as with student grading, a variety of criteria upon which to make judgments.

Student evaluations offer a good endpoint for our discussion. They form part of an overall pattern of relentless assessment of members of the academy. Graduate students/professors are evaluated by thesis committees, by anonymous "peers" for grant applications, for article submissions and, if lucky, by committees for tenure and promotion. The cycle is perpetual, and it moved Patricia Limerick Nelson to write caustically that "professors need more evaluations about as badly as Americans need more cholesterol."[103] Persistent review is worrisome because in a broad existential sense, it creates in the professoriate, tenured and untenured, the habit of seeing their self-worth through the eyes of others. This is dangerous on a personal level, because our actions and decisions may become "outer directed" (see Bridenbaugh's unfortunate statements in Chapter 2), based on external factors relating to the estimation of us by others. And this is dangerous pedagogically because our internal measure of ourselves, our comfort with who we are apart from outside judgment, transposes itself onto the courses we teach and makes us better instructors – and, ironically, more likely to be perceived positively.

---

103 Limerick, Aloof professors and shy students, p. 5.

4

The Historian and the Technological Revolution

In his famous essay "Motionless history," the Annaliste scholar Emmanuel LeRoy Ladurie called historians the "rear guard of the *avant-garde*." He noted how, as a group, historians leave the task "of carrying out the dangerous reconnaissance missions" to the "more sophisticated" disciplines and thus reap the fruits of someone else's hard labor.[1]

Nowhere is this more evident than with respect to technology. In the face of "an explosion" of online material and digital resources, historians move uncertainly forward, reexamining the ways they present materials to their students, as well as how they do their own research. They are often seen at the start of class apologizing to their students while they fumble with a computer, trying to get a recalcitrant PowerPoint or YouTube video to work.

The stakes are high. "History as a field of enquiry," says Toni Weller, "is standing on a conceptual precipice."[2] Technology is a flashpoint. It is the subject not only of potential embarrassment but of generational divides between older and younger faculty – what some have called the "chalk and talk" crowd and the "discovery and learning" crowd. In our graduate seminar at Vanderbilt, the topic was contentious. Surprisingly, student debate focused not on what technology to use but whether to use technology at all. This may seem unusual for a generation weaned on the internet but historians, budding and otherwise, are often text based, and indeed constitute a "rear guard" insofar as their perception of their discipline does not readily allow for modern technology.

---

1 Emmanual Le Roy Ladurie, Motionless history. *Social Science History*, 1:2 (Winter 1977), pp. 119–120.
2 Toni Weller, *History in the Digital Age* (Abingdon, UK: Routledge Press, 2013), p. 1.

"So if you don't mind, I'll just go ahead and read out each slide word for word in a droning monotone until you all yearn for the sweet release of death."

Source: Loren Fishman, Humoresque Cartoons

The potential perils and rewards are clear from the large and growing number of studies devoted to the subject. Cherie Kerr has accused educators of "killing softly" their students with uninspiring PowerPoint presentations. Rick Altman's succinctly titled *Why Most PowerPoint Presentations Suck* (2007) is now in its third edition. Thomas L. Russell speaks apocalyptically of "Technology Wars" (1997), while Gretchen Adams details a "Digital Revolution" (2011) in teaching history. Roy Rozensweig's influential collection of essays takes the provocative title *Clio Wired*, in reference to the effect of technology on the Greek goddess of history. From 2009 to 2012, the *Chronicle of Higher Education* published 95 articles on the digital humanities alone.[3]

---

3 Stephen Brier, Where's the Pedagogy? The Role of Teaching and Learning in the Digital Humanities. https://academicworks.cuny.edu/gc_pubs/201//

It may well be that we have already reached the revisionist stage of analysis. But the availability of digital sources and "big data" has generated fascinating possibilities for both teaching and researching history. The two endeavors are not, however, in synch and indeed, the differences lie at the root of much dramatic tension among historians.

An Ongoing Debate

What is immediately clear is that whatever technology one employs, the user must know how to work it. There is absolutely no excuse – however charming a professor's *mea culpas* may be – for delaying or interrupting a class with a technological struggle. It diverts student attention and makes creating a productive mood for learning more difficult. Students do not pay high tuitions to watch professors flounder. Faculty should arrive early to class and bring a plan B in case the equipment does not work.

It is in any case incorrect to assume that students are more tech savvy than their professors. Some students indeed are but many know only how to use their cell phones, social media, and online games. Therefore, it often does no good for professors to ask for help from the audience. In my experience, many students still prefer, where possible, to have course materials in printed form. During my tenure as director of undergraduate studies, I was surprised to find that the most common complaint from students was the lack of printed course catalogues, which they find easier to negotiate than the online version. The old format allowed them to see the whole set of course listings, the online version gives a partial page by page rendering. When asked why I had a printed book and they did not, I realized that my answer did not only involve perception of our relative skills with respect to technology, but likely economic considerations on the part of the university. It is cheaper to put it online.

Technology has nevertheless changed the classroom, both in terms of what we can do in it and the ways we can extend our pedagogical reach beyond the bricks and mortar walls. The first day of class now begins with the professor stating policies about use of electronic devices in class. We include the rules in our syllabi and reinforce them verbally to students during class, sometimes quite stridently. A colleague of mine calls this "unplugging" her class, removing competition for student attention. In that sense, it is a teacher's declaration of priority rather than strictly speaking a technological prohibition. The professor will use the computer at the front of the room to project images, maps, and texts. The classroom returns to its traditional equilibrium, with the teacher in charge of the message and its delivery. But the issue of use of computers has become more complicated as students have come to rely on them in secondary schools and arrive at college less able to perform simple tasks such as writing by hand. Thus, many professors focus their restrictions on cell phones.

Professional studies are divided on the efficacy of new technology. The title of Thomas Russell's book, *The No Significant Difference Phenomenon* (1999), makes clear his conclusion. Based on extensive study, Russell concluded that technology in the classroom "neither improves nor diminishes instruction for the masses."[4] He stressed, however, that technology is not neutral, but has different effects on different students. The real challenge facing educators is to identify student tendencies and match them with the appropriate technologies. Russell envisioned a variegated approach that combined older methods with newer ones. Alison Wolf in *Does Education Matter? Myths about Education and Economic Growth* (2002) noted that no matter what the means of delivery, the communication of ideas always remains strongly interpersonal. "We have not found any low cost, high technology alternatives to expert human teachers."[5] Patrik Svensson took a more ecumenical view in "Envisioning the digital humanities" (2012), asserting that information technology and digital humanities serve as a laboratory for thinking through the current state of pedagogy and the future of the humanities as a whole.[6]

In any case, predictions that technology will "overwhelm" the humanities and classroom teaching have been overstated. As Antonio Cantu and Wilson J. Warren point out in *Teaching History in the Digital Classroom* (2016), the art of prognosticating with respect to such things is inherently problematic. Thomas Edison predicted in 1922 that his new movie camera would revolutionize education and supplant textbooks.[7] It did not. Regardless of what the future brings, technology has at base forced professors to reexamine their pedagogical strategies. This is itself a worthwhile, albeit sometimes uncomfortable development. In addition, technology has facilitated the teaching of environmental history and materiality and allowed us to examine more closely the visual, spatial and aural dimensions of history and the connections among them. Technology is in fact encouraging the very type of interdisciplinarity that historians

---

4 Thomas Russell, *The No Significant Difference Phenomenon* (Raleigh: North Carolina State Press, 1999) and Technology wars: winners and losers. *Educom Review*, 32:2 (March/April 1997), pp. 23–24.
5 Alison Wolf, *Does Education Matter? Myths about Education and Economic Growth* (London: Penguin Books, 2002), p. 247.
6 Patrik Svensson, Envisioning the digital humanities. *Digital Humanities Quarterly*, 6 (2012). www.digitalhumanities.org/dhq/vol/6/1/000112/000112.html
7 D. Antonio Cantu and Wilson J. Warren, *Teaching History in the Digital Classroom* (Armonk: M. E. Sharpe, 2003), p. 2.

envisioned back in the 1960s and 1970s, but were not wholly able to deliver in a classroom setting.

Technology is, however, rapidly changing, as are the ideas of how to employ it effectively. All sides agree that it is necessary for teachers to find methods that are comfortable, that mesh with general pedagogical principles of intellectual engagement of students that stand at the core of all good teaching. In this regard, university teaching centers have become more important than ever as loci for the dissemination of new technology and teaching instructors how to use it. As my colleague, Ole Molvig, who uses technology expertly in his courses on the history of science, rightly asserts: students do not seek technological virtuosity in the first instance from professors, but rather clarity and engagement. There is no point in being part of the technological *avant-garde* for the sake of relevance or being on the correct side of the so-called pedagogical revolution. Jose Antonio Bowen's recent book, *Teaching Naked*, reminds us that technology is a tool and not in itself an education strategy.[8] And as Daniel Genkins, a post-doc at Brown University tasked with bridging the gap between programming and classroom deployment of technology, asserts, faculty must not be afraid to be innovative.[9]

In any case, it is important to avoid the all too common justification that technology bridges the gap between the world of the student and that of the professor. The notion is simplistic. It presupposes that students inhabit a single world that is inevitably foreign to us. It ignores a fundamental purpose of teaching: to push students beyond their supposed comfort zones, introduce them to what is unfamiliar and try to make them enjoy and appreciate it. The message is still more important in an increasingly global world. Rather than meditate on differences in world views, professors would do well to embrace the common sense of mutual discovery inherent in the pursuit of knowledge that unites teacher and student in the best possible way (see Chapter 1).

PowerPoint

Despite its uneven reputation in the literature, PowerPoint is alive and well in history classes. In its simplest application, it has replaced the maps that we used to carry under our arms to class, and the slide trays and projectors we brought to show images. PowerPoint maps and images

---

8 Jose Antonio Bowen, *Teaching Naked: How Moving Technology Out of Your College Classroom Will Improve Student Learning* (San Francisco: Jossey-Bass, 2012).
9 Interview with Daniel Genkins.

are far better than the old ones. They can be interactive and juxtapose different types of maps and images from different eras to facilitate comparison over time. They can demonstrate the spatial layout of cities and rural regions, and the relationships between the one and the other.

Indeed, rather than opposing older methods, PowerPoint in fact reinforces the type of investigation that historians envisioned back in the nineteenth century (see Chapter 2). Wilhelm Putz's much used and much disliked textbook *Ancient History and Geography* (1846) argued, as the title suggests, for an intrinsic link between geography and historical analysis. Putz believed that historical study of ancient Greek democracy could properly proceed only with an understanding of Greece's mountainous terrain, lack of hinterland, and small urban space that brought people face to face and facilitated intellectual exchange. Arnold Toynbee stressed a strikingly similar point in his famous *magnum opus* (similarly ignored nowadays), *A Study of History*. Toynbee compared the "rocky," "bony" and otherwise inhospitable landscape of intellectually vibrant Athens to the fertile rural lands of intellectually "backward" Boeotia, whose people were the butt of jokes by Greek playwrights.[10] New sophisticated maps allow teachers to show clearly these stark environmental differences. I juxtapose images of Athens and Boeotia in Western Civilization as a prelude to discussion of Athens and reading Aristophanes' *Lysistrata*. Aristophanes enjoyed making fun of rustic folk.

PowerPoint has proved useful not only for maps and images, but also for the presentation of written texts. Professor Samantha Kelly of Rutgers University admits that although she had heard about all the faults of PowerPoint, she found that it worked particularly well in her large classes. It allowed students to read the texts projected in front of the room together with her, even if they had not done so before class. She saw it as promoting a productive "group analysis."[11] The inhibitions of the large lecture hall were reduced and students felt more free to comment and the professor better able to discuss detail. The instructor could also see more easily who was engaged, and, with a well-placed stare, redirect wandering eyes. Corey Tazzara finds that PowerPoint is similarly effective in his small seminars at Scripps College. Apart from projecting the reading material in front of the students, it helps change the "tempo and energy" of the classroom and "appeals to more visual learners."[12]

As many of my colleagues readily point out, close reading of historical texts can be done without PowerPoint. They require their students to

---

10 Arnold J Toynbee, *A Study of History* (abridged by D.C. Somerville, vols I–VI) (Oxford: Oxford University Press, 1987), pp. 89–90.
11 Interview with Samantha Kelly.
12 Interview with Corey Tazzara.

bring the materials to class and go over them closely. I have done this myself (see Chapter 3) before the advent of PowerPoint. Professors call on students to read aloud, which similarly alters the tempo of the class and facilitates close text-based discussion (see Chapter 3). The routine has the additional benefit of promoting responsibility: students must bring their books to class. They are also encouraged to listen to each other, which is not a given. Years of secondary education have often reinforced the notion among students that the teacher is the bearer of knowledge and insight. Mutual possession of a physical source helps alter the dynamic.

It is again important not to suppose that "old school" methods and "new technology" are mutually exclusive. One may show PowerPoint slides and still ask students to bring in the book or printed versions of the reading to class. The approaches do not have to overlap. The printed materials are often long and cannot be easily transferred to a screen. When brought to class, students and teachers can move from one passage to another in different parts of the work, reading aloud, juxtaposing themes and ideas. I have found PowerPoint particularly useful for short, unfamiliar medieval primary source materials. *Commenda* contracts are, for example, the driest of medieval documents. They are, however, critical to understanding premodern trade and the development of credit. When projected onto a screen, student attention is drawn to the arcane language of the document, which contains obscure references to monetary units and invocations of God that students ignore for the sake of ascertaining basic meaning. Projection makes these impossible to ignore. It provokes questions that I had previously discreetly avoided for the sake of simple explication of premodern credit. But in this format, students want to know what the monetary units mean, how much they were worth, did medieval people really have these sums and why are there references to God in a credit instrument that presumably shows the secular side of medieval society?

Students are, as Sam Wineberg advises, thinking like historians, contextualizing the primary source, and trying to link it with other facts they know.[13] This facilitates discussion of the material circumstances of medieval people, the meaning of money (which then, unlike today, had intrinsic worth), the manner of medieval accounting and the nature of Christianity, which indeed played an important role in the financial sphere. The students ponder how seemingly discreet parts of a distant society are connected. Is it possible to separate economy from faith in the

---

13 Sam Wineberg, Thinking like a historian. *Teaching with Primary Sources Quarterly*, 3:1 (Winter 2010). www.loc.gov/teachers/tps/quarterly/historical_thinking/pdf/historical_thinking.pdf

Middle Ages, or is this imposing a modernity onto the distant past? Such questions have been otherwise difficult for me to address in abstract terms.

The example supports T. Mills Kelly's assertion that the internet helps bring history alive for students. But his conclusion, that students would otherwise be condemned to endure the unproductive "sit, listen and record" method of the earlier generation, should be modified.[14] Jennifer Spock, who makes frequent use of PowerPoint in her overcrowded classes at Eastern Kentucky University, argues that "the basics still apply even if the vehicle changes."[15] Students still must pay attention and take notes and, on that basis, formulate considered responses and opinions. Technology without the human element is likely the most ineffective pedagogy of all. The medium in any case matters less than the message. The key for instructors is finding an attractive and congenial form of engagement suited to all participants.

Professors find additional utility in PowerPoint for its capacity to make available class presentations and lectures in advance so that students may consult them at home and reserve problem solving for the class meeting. Most colleges and universities now have internal online delivery systems, where students and faculty can interact. At Vanderbilt, we have used "Oak," "Blackboard" and now "Brightspace" as our systems – each more sophisticated than the last. Syllabi with online readings can be accessed with a stroke of a key. Many of my colleagues have, however, been reluctant to post lecture presentations online for fear that students will be less likely to come to class. I myself fear this because students have told me they do it.

What emphatically does not work in any context is the use of PowerPoint images as a casual backdrop to lectures. The quick flash of an image on the screen while the instructor says the name or concept (behold Martin Luther!) is distracting. A case study by Yukiko Inoue-Smith (2016) indicates that students feel overwhelmed by "rapid fire" PowerPoint images.[16] Slides that show the words that will be spoken verbally in the lecture can also be distracting. PowerPoint is at its best when the image projected is directly referred to and explicated by the speaker and discussed with the students.

---

14 T. Mills Kelly, *Teaching History in the Digital Age* (Ann Arbor: University of Michigan Press, 2013), p. 12.
15 Interview with Jennifer Spock.
16 Yukiko Inoue-Smith, College-based case studies in using PowerPoint effectively. *Cogent Education*, 3 (2016). www.tandfonline.com/doi/full/10.1080/2331186X.2015.1127745

Cherie Kerr in her indictment of PowerPoint argues that "slimming down" and making PowerPoint less cluttered allows the presenter to get more into detail, which she sees as a prerequisite for success.[17] Kerr urges users to be creative, take risks and even "follow the mindset of an improv comic." It is unclear how the last suggestion fits the agendas of most professional historians.[18] And subjects like art history clearly require numerous images. But creativity (short of improv) is helpful for the examination of images. The deployment of additional technological features, such as fade-ins and -outs and multiple screens, is effective if the material is directly discussed. If left to do the work alone, however, the pyrotechnics can detract from the message and analysis; more than a few recent job talks have failed on this type of one-sided technological creativity. As Inoue-Smith found, PowerPoint is good for visually "enriching content and illustrating complex concepts" but it is "not good at providing large amounts of information."

The possibilities are nevertheless exciting. For a lecture entitled "Early Modern Nations and Statecraft," in my Western Civilization class, I now show an image of Hans Holbein's *The Ambassadors* and ask students to unpack what they see on screen. With high-resolution pictures and fade-in technology, I can highlight the details of the painting, focus on its intentionally contradictory features, and compare them with material objects of the era. When our discussion uncovers relevant themes, I begin my lecture on those terms. What was for many years a bad lecture that I dreaded has been transformed into one that, if nothing else, gains the students' attention. I glance around the room and the students are looking at me.

YouTube/Wikipedia/Blogs

A friend of mine in secondary school was fond of posing a hypothetical question. "What do teachers do when they have no time to prepare and have nothing to say?" They show movies.

If the lecture, as some argue, is a passive form of learning, what then does one say of film? Students sit and listen with the lights out? The only thing lacking is a pillow.

Jonathan Rees, a historian at Colorado State University at Pueblo, tells of holding a similar prejudice against film. Nevertheless, he was among

---

17 Cherie Kerr, *Death by Powerpoint: How to Avoid Killing your Presentation and Sucking the Life Out of the Audience* (Santa Ana: Execuprov Press, 2001).
18 Kerr, *Death by Powerpoint*, pp. 84–87.

the first group of historians to use YouTube in his classes and quickly came to appreciate its virtues. YouTube provides short clips that can, like written texts, be explicated carefully and collectively as they are being shown. Rees used a two-minute video from the movie *The Grapes of Wrath* to illustrate the plight of sharecroppers during the Great Depression and the famous Daisy Ad used by Lyndon Johnson's presidential campaign in 1964 to scare voters about possible nuclear disaster if his opponent won the election.[19]

Lendol Calder put it well when he wrote in 2006 that a carefully chosen film clip can help a student "take an empathetic leap into the past."[20] Richard Davis of Bard College sees YouTube as a good way to introduce students to unfamiliar Indian Bhakti devotional poetry. He shows performances to provide direct experience that improves understanding and appreciation of the written primary sources.[21] Neslihan Senocak of Columbia University uses the YouTube video "Into Great Silence," a recent German film set at a monastery in the Alps, to introduce students to the unfamiliar world of medieval Carthusian monasticism.

The empathetic leap can be humorous. My colleague Catherine Molineux shows an animated video of the English Bayeux tapestry in a class on British history. The video scans the tapestry and, with a light touch, puts the figures into motion. It gives a real sense of the Norman Invasion, with ships sailing the channel, horses moving forward to battle. It accentuates the meaning of the tapestry, which is otherwise rendered in single stationary (and partial) images. We laughed together watching it, and I decided to try the video in my classes. It is the equivalent of reading a primary source document. I stopped the video at various parts to ask questions about it. It has worked well despite my initial misgivings about the genre.

If historians have moved cautiously with YouTube, they have been outright hostile to Wikipedia. The ubiquitous online entries, with their brief summaries of people and events, have become a standard source for historical facts. For current students, who grew up with it, Wikipedia is often the first place they look for information. For professional historians and university teachers, however, Wikipedia is famously problematic. It lacks the rigorous peer review of published books, which are carefully vetted for accuracy. This is true despite the so-called "talk page," where editors discuss changes and show additions and deletions

---

19 Jonathan Rees, Teaching history with YouTube. *Perspectives on History* (2008), p. 30.
20 Lendol Calder, Uncoverage: toward a signature pedagogy. *Journal of American History*, 92 (2006), p. 1364.
21 Interview with Richard Davis.

to Wikipedia entries. The shortcomings induced the history department at Middlebury College in 2007 to ban students from citing Wikipedia as a source in all papers.[22]

The problem is not with Wikipedia per se, however, but with its use for historical research. Historians worry not only about the veracity of the facts but about the students' tendency to assume that facts are already settled and may be accessed uncritically with a stroke of a computer key. In this regard, Wikipedia reinforces the "referential illusion" of historical facts that is the antagonist to critical, historical (and unnatural) thinking.

But attitudes toward the use of Wikipedia in history classrooms are changing. Roy Rosenzweig, the late director of the Center for History and New Media at George Mason University, credited Wikipedia (and the internet in general) with decentralizing knowledge and creating a public space, available to all, that has opened up "new possibilities for collaboration between student and professor that did not previously exist."[23] In an essay for *The Journal of American History*, Rosenzweig argued that many Wikipedia entries are in fact more accurate than their counterparts in traditional encyclopedias. He saw the real issue as making clear to students that Wikipedia must not to be confused with critical historical thinking.[24]

Accordingly, historians have begun accommodating Wikipedia in their classes, using it as a learning tool rather than as an alternative source of historical facts. Kevin Sheets, a historian at the University of New York at Cortland, uses Wikipedia to "enliven" a previously "unpopular" historical methodology course.[25] Sheets created a project called "CortlandWiki," which required students to go to local archives and collectively write a Wikipedia entry for the history of the town of Cortland. The first step was for the students to write a conventional 8–10-page paper on the subject from traditional published sources. The next step involved creating a "Wiki space" online and adding posts from their research. The students then modified the posts, editing each other's work and adding more information. Sheets tells of substantial arguments among the students, who did not agree on what needed to be

---

22 Scott Jaschik, A stand against Wikipedia. *Inside Higher Education* (January 26 2007). www.insidehighered.com/news/2007/01/26/stand-against-wikipedia
23 Roy Rosenzweig, *Clio Wired: The Future of the Past in the Digital Age* (New York: Columbia University Press, 2011).
24 Kevin Sheets, Wiki in the classroom: can joint-authoring technology help students understand the nature of the historian's craft? *Perspectives on History*, 47 (May 2009), pp. 52–54.
25 Roy Rosenzweig, Can history be open source? Wikipedia and the future of the past. *Journal of American History*, 93 (June 2006), pp. 117–146.

included and how the material should be cast. The students enjoyed picking apart the prose and ideas of others and, conversely, were offended when their own contributions were modified. What developed from the exercise was active engagement in, and conversation about, the past and how historians decide what matters historically. The students participated in the process of historical inquiry, which they had previously found difficult to appreciate.

A challenge with such assignments is making sure that the technology itself is readily usable and comprehensible to students. To facilitate this, there are websites, including from the so-called Wiki Education Foundation, that explain the nuances of the technology and how to avoid glitches that could stymie classes.[26] The presumption again is that students are not tech experts, and the professor must, as much as possible, understand how to deploy the medium.

Perhaps the greatest benefit of having students write Wikipedia entries is that it gives them a sense of urgency about their assignments. The fact that students' work will be seen by the outside world raises the stakes and, indeed, makes the assignment resemble more closely the work of their professors. The "public" for whom the students are writing is in fact larger than that of their professors. For this reason, Dariusz Jemielniak, author of the recent *Common Knowledge? An Ethnography of Wikipedia*, calls Wikipedia a professor's "best friend." "If you're writing something millions of people are going to read, it's a reason to do a really good job, to go into a library and get a deep understanding of the topic."[27] Tamar Carroll, a historian in the Women's Studies department at Rochester Institute of Technology, reports that students viewed her assignment – a Wikipedia entry for Mary Stafford Anthony, the suffragist and sister of Susan B. Anthony – as "among the most meaningful assignments" they had during their entire undergraduate careers. She found that the "talk page" of the Wikipedia entry was useful in getting students to understand the give and take involved in the process of writing history.

T. Mills Kelly of George Mason University took teaching the historical process with Wikipedia to an entirely new level in 2008. He taught a class called "Lying about History" (History 389), which required his students to set up a fictitious Wikipedia page for a pirate named Edward Owens. The hoax is now famous. The students mixed facts with falsehoods and even set up a YouTube video dedicated to Owens. The page went viral and was taken by readers as real. The vicissitudes of the fakery were later revealed in an article in *The Atlantic*. Professor Kelly explained his

---

26 https://wikiedu.org
27 Dariusz Jemielniak, Wikipedia, a professor's best friend. *Chronicle of Higher Education* (October 13 2014). www.chronicle.com/article/wikipedia-a-professors-best/149337

rationale. "By learning about historical fakery," students became "much better consumers of historical information."[28]

A similar rationale lies behind the use of blogging. The online activity has long been popular with people seeking to express their thoughts and opinions to the outside world. Recently, it has been employed as a learning tool in history classrooms. Professors use it as a species of online diary that requires students to make daily entries and thus write more frequently. The assignment is similar to the writing journals employed by Professor Mary Sheldon Barnes at turn of the twentieth century Wellesley College (see Chapter two). It differs, however, in that student efforts are placed into the public sphere.[29]

As with Wikipedia, teachers and student must familiarize themselves with the technology, which includes creating a platform to build a blog site using edublog.com or blogspot.com. The pedagogical value of blogging is peer interaction and collaboration. In his "Methods of Historical Research and Writing" class at Eastern Michigan University, Russell Olwell requires his students to work together on a blog focused on the historical theme of "Veterans and Oral History." He bases the assignment on a book called *Patriots: An Oral History of the Vietnam War from All Sides* written by Chris Appy. The students correspond directly with the author of the book. The advantage, Olwell asserts, is that it makes students take history more personally. Direct communication with the author gives them a better sense of the historian's task.

The downside to the course is that what an author says about his work and what the work itself says are not necessarily the same thing. One does not need to be Jacques Derrida to appreciate the difference between a writer's intention and message. The Teaching Resource Center at University of Michigan makes the important point that professors who use blogs must follow the "traditional rules" for all assignments. They should make clear at the start the expectations and state them verbally and on the syllabus. The Center also recommends dividing students into small groups, preferably less than ten, and allotting a specific amount of time for posts and for commenting on each other's work. The routine allows students to get to know each other and their respective writing

---

28 Yoni Applebaum, How the professor who fooled Wikipedia got caught by Reddit. *The Atlantic* (March 15 2012). www.theatlantic.com/technology/archive/2012/05/how-the-professor-who-fooled-wikipedia-got-caught-by-reddit/257134/
29 Russell Olwell, Taking history personally: how blogs connect students outside the classroom. *Perspectives on History* (January 2008). www.historians.org/publications-and-directories/perspectives-on-history/january-2008/taking-history-personally-how-blogs-connect-students-outside-the-classroom

styles, while reducing the stress for the instructor by creating order and ensuring that all students receive comments. [30]

Digital Humanities

No technological sector is growing faster and has garnered more attention recently than the digital humanities. The term itself requires explanation. The distinction between it and basic online sources is not entirely clear. Toni Weller in *History in the Digital Age* places email and the internet under the rubric of "digital resources." William G. Thomas III, a historian at University of Nebraska and a pioneer in the field, defines digital humanities as "new communication technologies of the computer."[31] Brett Bobley, director of the NEH's Office of Digital Humanities, said in a radio interview in January 2011 that "digital humanities is really applying digital technology to doing traditional study."[32] He argued also that digitizing books, manuscripts, and primary source materials and making them available online would revolutionize the way historians go about their craft.

The revolution, whatever its exact nature, is in full swing. Schools have set up centers for digital humanities, aided by funding from the Mellon Foundation. They provide short-term jobs for postdoctoral students. UCLA's digital humanities program offers a minor for undergraduates and a certificate for graduates. It stresses the role of digital resources in expanding the "reach and impact of the humanities" for the "sake of the public good," a purpose that, as we have seen in Chapter 2, has traditionally been assigned to history. The University of Nebraska offers a class called "Digital History" for both undergraduates and graduates. The stated rationale is "to develop expertise in the theories and tools of digital scholarship." In 2007, a journal, *Digital Humanities Quarterly*, based at Brown University, was begun to relay developments in the field.

Digital humanities is now, in Patrik Svensson's estimation, "a big tent of inclusivity" for the humanities.[33] The definition remains vague but the major concern is how to deploy it effectively in the classroom. Steven

---

30 https://lsa.umich.edu/sweetland/instructors/teaching-resources/using-blogs-in-the-classroom.html

31 William G. Thomas III, Interchange, the promise of digital history. *Journal of American History* (September 2008), p. 454.

32 "Interview with Brett Bobley of the Office for Digital Humanities at the NEH. https://blogs.loc.gov/thesignal/2011/10/interview-with-brett-bobley/

33 Patrik Svensson, Envisioning the digital humanities, and Beyond the big tent, in: *Debates in the Digital Humanities,* edited by Matthew K. Gold (Minneapolis: University of Minnesota Press, 2012). See also in same volume, Tara McPherson, Why Are the digital humanities so white? or Thinking the histories of race and computation.

Brier of the City University of New York asks pointedly: "Where's the pedagogy?"[34] Svensson argued that the utility lay in the "predominantly textual orientation" of digital humanities, which matches the basic goals of history and "facilitates teaching interdisciplinary fields such as Africana studies and gender studies." T. Mills Kelly views digital humanities as a means of bridging the gap between the everyday activities of students and their studies. It serves as a "venture in" for students to look more closely at subject fields.

William G. Thomas III of Nebraska and Ed Ayers of the University of Virginia taught a series of seminars using digital sources consisting of letters written by participants in the American Civil War. The goal of the class was to get students to assess "what aspects of the letters were most important." The students worked in groups and gave public demonstrations on the Web at the end of the semester. One group produced a site devoted to "U.S. Colored Troops." It generated questions from outsiders, to whom the students responded. Professor Thomas described this "interactive engagement" as the fundamental virtue of the class.[35]

The digitized materials have opened new possibilities for reading and intellectual inquiry. In 2014, a consortium including Johns Hopkins' Sheridan libraries, the Princeton University Library and University College London's Centre for Editing Lives and Letters (CELL) in collaboration with professors Lisa Jardine and Anthony Grafton implemented "The Archaeology of Reading in Early Modern Europe" program (see Chapter 3). The website contains marked-up old manuscripts and books, with the owners' notes in the margins. It allows scholars and students to explore how people read in the past, what caught their eye and how they responded to it. The interactive features allow investigators to look at details of texts and juxtapose different parts. As a teaching tool, looking at marginalia, even if it is not easily comprehended, makes its own point to the students and stimulates discussion. The very image of the old texts gives teachers a chance to share with their students a private joy of their work –the appearance of the times, which helped inspire many of us to study history in the first place.

Historians have expressed similar enthusiasm for emerging geographic information systems (GIS) technology. GIS works on the same principle as the global positioning devices used in cars. It consists of software that provides a location on the earth. It is interactive: users can pose questions and receive visual responses. Historians have employed GIS in their

34 Brier, Where's the Pedagogy? https://academicworks.cuny.edu/gc_pubs/201/
35 William G. Thomas III, Computing and the historical imagination. In: *A Companion to Digital Humanities,* edited by Susan Schreibman, Ray Siemens and John Unsworth (Maldon: Blackwell, 2004), pp. 56–67.

research to examine issues relating to population, health, employment, climate, and crime patterns. The technology allows detailed modeling of geography, including road networks and buildings. In this respect, it has greatly facilitated a spatial turn in historical study.[36] David J Bodenhamer, a pioneer in the field, notes that GIS allows historians to reimagine and even recreate lost places.[37] They can compare geographic data from Great Britain to Tibet, from Peru to Tokyo.

From the perspective of the university classroom, the technology is particularly useful given the notorious ignorance of students with regard to geography – a problem that has ironically grown worse in recent years owing to this same GIS technology in smart phones. But as a teaching tool, GIS facilitates presentation of detailed images of landscapes and geographical formations. Jill S. Harris, a professor of economics at Pitzer College, has found GIS helpful especially in discussions of statistical and theoretical information. It allows her in her macroeconomics class to avoid bland statements like "unemployment was rising in the USA" and to refer students instead to a GIS thematic map, with geocoded data, that gives the ZIP codes of unemployed workers. It shows visually how trends vary from county to county across the country. The presentation makes a far greater impression on students and elicits more spirited discussions.[38]

Open enrollment colleges have, as noted in Chapter 3, often been at the forefront of technological innovation in the classroom. The City University of New York (CUNY) with its 260,000 students, many of whom come from working-class backgrounds, is a leader in the use of digital technology. The large number of students pressured the institution to manage classes in creative ways. In the 1990s, Stephen Brier and Roy Rosenzweig put together a course called *Who Built America* that employed what was then the latest technology available, including CD-ROMs with films, text, audio and visual images. The aim of the class was to place social history, especially labor history, at the center of American history. The CD-ROM won a prize in 1994 from the American Historical Association and a reviewer called it a "massive tour-de-force" that made the study of labor accessible to a broad swathe of students. In 2009, CUNY went forward again, creating the Academic Commons (AC),

---

36 David J. Bodenheimer, The spatial humanities: space, time, and place in the new digital age. In: Toni Weller, *History in the Digital Age* (New York: Routledge, 2013), pp. 23–38.

37 *The Spatial Humanities: GIS and the Future of Humanities Scholarship*, edited by David J. Bodenhamer, John Corrigan, and Trevor M. Harris (Bloomington: Indiana University Press, 2010).

38 Jill S. Harris, Using GIS to teach economics education: evidence of increasing returns to scale (July 2010). https://ssrn.com/abstract=1984971

initiated by George Otte and Matthew K. Gold. This is a platform for scholarly communication across all of CUNY's branches that brings together academics working with digital technologies and pedagogies under a single digital umbrella. It has become a paradigm that is being replicated at other colleges and will no doubt continue to evolve.

MOOCs and Online Classes

The technological revolution has, however, not been consistent. One of the more complicated developments has been the advent of online and "massive open online" courses (MOOCs). In 2011, 6.7 million American students were enrolled in at least one online course. The number includes those studying at for-profit colleges, which often conduct classes solely on the web. The courses fit the irregular schedules of nontraditional students, who often work full time and have families, and in this sense have helped, as some observers note, to "democratize" education

Online classes began in the early 2000s.[39] They offer full credit and students pay for them like traditional college classes. MOOCs, on the other hand, are free to all students and are generated by private companies like Coursera, who profit from them. The classes usually do not count toward a degree, although some offer certificates of completion. They differ from online courses also in that assessment of student work is computer based, while online courses are more interactive and involve feedback directly from a professor.

For all their technological sophistication, MOOCs in their first iteration closely resembled the lecture classes of the late nineteenth century. The irony is self-evident since, as we saw in Chapter 3, the recent pedagogical literature has generally condemned the lecture as a passive form of learning and opposed it to active learning. The MOOC was still worse. It was a lecture lacking both the physical presence of the lecturer, and thus interaction with students, and assessment of their comprehension of the material!

Cold-hearted business realities lay behind the development. MOOCS offered financial benefits for universities and the companies that oversee them.[40] An article in business-friendly *Forbes* magazine (March 2017) argued in favor of MOOCs on the grounds that they "reduce the need for

---

39 *Macro-Level Learning through Massive Open Online Courses (MOOCs): Strategies*, edited by Elspeth McKay and John Lenarcic (Hershey: IGI Global, 2015).
40 Burck Smith, Let's deregulate online learning. *Chronicle of Higher Education* (November 2011). www.chronicle.com/article/Lets-Deregulate-Online/129617

infrastructure and classrooms" and thus "achieve optimal resource utilization." The sonorous statement was music to the ears of CEOs and university administrators. To be fair, the essay also points out credible intellectual benefits, such as having "a Nobel prize winning scholar" teach thousands rather than the hundreds of students she/he would otherwise reach in a physical classroom.[41] Everybody wins! Select faculty go "viral" on the internet and universities make money!

But there has been an ongoing reexamination of the pedagogical utility of MOOCs and online classes more generally. A poll of professors done by the journal *Inside Higher Education* in 2016 showed that only one in five believe that such courses achieve student learning outcomes equivalent to those of in-person courses. Jeremy Adelman of Princeton University, a pioneer of MOOCs with his course on Latin American history, complained that although the class was designed to "maximize scale and reception," it lacked sufficient "collaborative learning" to be effective and indeed only "replicated older conventions of teaching." "Planet MOOC," as he called it, was "underpopulated" when he fashioned his course in 2013. It now resembles the cluttered "São Paulo skyline." Adelman believed that students fell into "passive learning practices" and suggested that "version 3.0" of MOOCs include assignment of more frequent papers and greater interaction so that "online learners can team up to produce materials for everyone else in the course."[42]

Other historians have expressed similarly conflicted opinions. They question the type of courses universities make available and even the process by which these decisions are made by administrators. In an essay in *Perspectives on History* (March 2013), John McNeill, a historian at Georgetown University, offered both a "Dystopian" and "Utopian" view of MOOCs. In the first instance, their popularity would result in fewer academic historians working on research. According to the second, professors would, conversely, have more time for research. He asked the uncomfortable question: if successful teaching can be delivered via MOOCs, why should colleges and universities employ historians to both teach and do research?[43] Ellen Wexler in a recent essay in *The Chronicle of Higher Education* emphasized only the negative aspects. She argued

---

41 Deepa Mehta, The future of massively open online courses (MOOCs). *Forbes* (March 2017). www.forbes.com/sites/quora/2017/03/23/the-future-of-massively-open-online-courses-moocs/#a8bd90f6b830
42 Jeremy Adelman, History a la MOOC, Version 2.0. *Perspectives on History* (2014). www.historians.org/publications-and-directories/perspectives-on-history/february-2014/history-a-la-mooc-version-20
43 John McNeill, MOOCs and historical research. *Perspectives on History* (2013). www.historians.org/publications-and-directories/perspectives-on-history/march-2013/moocs-and-historical-research

that watching a video lecture without interactive engagement is simply "a bad way to learn." She cited a study done by researchers at Carnegie Mellon University, whose title makes clear the conclusion: "Learning is not a spectator sport: doing is better than watching from a MOOC."[44]

Nevertheless, it is important to repeat the caveat from Chapter 2. The lecture as a model and moving image, as it were, of intellectual engagement and thus inspiration for study is too easily dismissed. It is possible even via the net to inspire minds to the type of lifelong independent study that educators seek.

And there are excellent examples of online teaching, which is becoming the norm in universities rather than the exception. They are associated in the first instance with for-profit schools like University of Phoenix, a pioneer in the 1990s, lacking bricks and mortar structures and a permanent workforce.[45] The National Education Association issued guidelines in 2003, suggesting skills and requirements for effective online instruction, which included instructors sharing as much face-to-face computer interaction as possible.[46] But although for-profits have failed in recent years, the online course has remained. Traditional colleges and universities entered the online business, sensing economic advantages and aided by charitable organizations such ad the Alfred P. Sloan Foundation. New York University established a for-profit online sector in 1998, followed by numerous other institutions.[47] There are a host of university web pages that provide instruction for online teachers, who are drawn both from the regular faculty and from adjuncts.[48] Instructional advisors help faculty design courses. Brown University's Best Practices of Teaching Online advises teachers to establish a teacherly presence by means of discussion forums and "posting the interests" of students in the form of biographical information.[49] Arizona State University, which has one of the nation's largest online programs, offers workshops four times a year for some 400 instructors, who can view online tutorials and live webcasts, as well as

44 Ellen Wexler, In online courses, students learn more by doing than by watching. *Chronicle of Higher Education* (September 2016). www.chronicle.com/blogs/wiredcampus/in-online-courses-students-learn-more-by-doing-than-by-watching/57365

45 Ryan Craig. A brief history (and future) of on-line degrees. www.forbes.com/sites/ryancraig/2015/06/23/a-brief-history-and-future-of-online-degrees/#22934d6c48d9

46 www.nea.org/assets/docs/onlineteachguide.pdf

47 Hope Kentnor, Distance education and the evolution of online learning in the United States. https://digitalcommons.du.edu/cgi/viewcontent.cgi?article=1026&context=law_facpub

48 www.umass.edu/oapa/sites/default/files/pdf/handbooks/teaching_and_learning_online_handbook.pdf

49 www.brown.edu/academics/professional/faculty/online/best-practices.php

exchange ideas and information. Marc Van Horn, ASU's chief online learning officer, said that the most important aspect of teaching online classes is that instructors understand as much as possible what it is like to be an online student.[50] *US News and World Report* has even begun to rate online programs. In 2018, Ohio State came out on top. It earned its rating on account of the quality of faculty and level of interaction among faculty and students and among students themselves.

The distinguished scholar Lynn Hunt provides an important perspective on what it is like for a successful career classroom instructor to teach an online course [51] She offered an online version of "Introduction to Western Civilization from 1715 to the Present" at UCLA, working closely with course developers from the Department of Film, Television, and Digital Media. She sat before a blank screen at a table under bright lights, unable to read the reaction of an audience, which was "unnerving." She worried about appearing disembodied and lacking direct contact with the students. But she found that the product was "remarkably personal." Skillful editing enhanced the visual and aural components of her lectures and even added features not possible in standard lecture format, such as visual overlay and captions. It had the benefit that students whose first language was not English could replay the lecture. Each week students wrote 250-word response papers to the readings and lecture, responded to each other's posts and wrote to the TAs and professors. Hunt points out that student opinion about the class was strikingly positive, especially for the "accessibility of the professor," one of the issues she worried about most.

The View from the Front of the Class

Lynn Hunt notes that her class was expensive to produce and that not all schools have the resources of UCLA. What is nevertheless clear is that technology has encouraged historians to rethink their methods and to experiment. Nearly all US universities now have online systems that allow exchange between professors and students beyond the physical classroom. Professors can post readings and syllabi and communicate with students. Merely having a syllabus online, as noted earlier, has the practical advantage of allowing students to access internet readings with a single click.

---

50 Jean Dimeo, Teaching teachers to teach online (October 11 2017). www.insidehighered.com/digital-learning/article/2017/10/11/how-colleges-train-instructors-teach-online-courses
51 Lynn Hunt, Teaching an on-line course. *Common Knowledge*, 24:3 (2018), pp. 397–401.

And from a medievalist's perspective, the internet makes available sources that were previously hard to find or exorbitantly expensive to buy.

Whatever technology professors use, they must acquaint themselves carefully with it. This requires time, which few scholars have in abundance. When Kathryn Reyerson, a medievalist at University of Minnesota, decided to enliven her large lecture course on medieval cities with new technology, she hired a graduate student and two educational technology consultants to work with her for nine months to produce a plan.[52] Reyerson decided to have students use clickers, hand-held devices, to register their reactions to the material, giving them a voice in the large crowd while allowing them to retain their anonymity. She used mapping technology and put students in groups together to physically recreate a medieval city. The class was transformed into an active laboratory for collective learning.

Careful deployment of technology improved old strategies and facilitated new ones. Samuel K. Cohn, a historian at the University of Glasgow, shared, albeit reluctantly, his extensive database on medieval wills with his class. One student complained that she took the course "precisely to avoid computers and statistics." She subsequently found the material so engaging that she decided to go to graduate school in digital humanities.[53]

Technology won over a skeptic. But we should nevertheless take care with current claims for the technological "revolution." The learning process depends on many factors, including, as noted in Chapter 3, a "socializing" process based on personal interactions between students and their friends and family as well as the overall atmosphere at the school they attend.[54] Professors must guard against the fiction that using the internet is equivalent to engaging students on their own terms. This involves the false assumption that students represent a distinct monolithic species, which I personally do not believe, and that tapping into their "world view" is essential to our effectiveness as teachers. In the same way that historians recognize common aspects of the human condition that link the present day to the distant past, we recognize common human elements that link us with the students we teach.

By way of conclusion, I wish to stress this last point. The rationale behind T. Mills Kelly's fake Wikipedia page class at George Mason University was to make students "more discerning consumers" of

---

52 Kathryn Reyerson, Kevin Mummey, and Jude Higdon, Medieval cities of Europe: click, tweet, map, and present. *History Teacher*, 44:3 (2011), p. 355.
53 Interview with Samuel K. Cohn.
54 Daniel F. Chambliss, Doing what works: on the mundanity of excellence in teaching. In: *The Social Worlds of Higher Education*, edited by Bernice Pescosolido and Ronald Aminzade (Thousand Oaks:, Pine Forge Press, 1999), p. 425.

historical information. The goal is laudable, and undoubtedly effective in Kelly's hands at promoting critical thinking. Less laudable, however, is Kelly's further justification that his approach counters the tendency among historians "to take an overly stuffy approach to the past" and make history "too boring for its own good."[55] The "digital realm," Kelly claims, not only prepares students for future careers, but it produces work that can "go viral" and get a "buzz." The goal undoubtedly sits well with students and their parents but it begs the basic question raised throughout this book: what exactly is the purpose of historical study? The assumption that historian/professors inevitably take "an overly stuffy approach to the past" is a cliché and the ability to fashion elaborate hoaxes to create an internet "buzz" is not the type of professional or personal quality I hope my students will take with them from college. Purposeful deception mirrors too closely the unfortunate features of the world that we currently live in. Indeed, is this really the "critical thinking" that scholars of pedagogy envision or is it just the opposite? The wisdom of Kelly's approach is still more troubling given that so many history majors go on to law and business school.

The foregoing discussion raises a still more existential issue. Technology has not only altered approaches to teaching classes at universities but, more importantly, it has altered the basic conception of reality in the world we inhabit. Indeed, this may well be the single greatest difference between the current generation of college students and previous generations. When I was a college student in the late 1970s and early 1980s, that which was physically in front of me was reality. I went to class with no email messages waiting for me, no electronic devices in hand, only a Timex watch on my wrist. My sense of an alternate realm was restricted to a phone call that I had perhaps received earlier and needed to return, or some prior conversation that had vexed me. Walking to class was a pastoral activity, occasionally shared with friends with whom I chatted. Nowadays, students – and human beings of all generations – operate on numerous levels of reality at once. Students come to class engaged in ongoing and unfinished conversations via email, Snapchat, Facebook, Instagram and other forms of social media. As a result, they project, by necessity, numerous personas at once. A walk is an opportunity to multitask: text friends, catch up on messages, google something for curiosity's sake. There are multiple realities, the physical surroundings of the campus being just one of them. From the perspective of pedagogy, this means that the student who stands before you is also floating about in some alternate universe that we do not see. This renders all the more important the need for a direct interaction between student and teacher.

---

55 Weller, *History in the Digital Age*, p. 13.

5

The Historian and the Academy

> The university, like all other human institutions, like the church, like governments, like philanthropic organizations, is not outside, but inside the general social fabric ... It is not something apart, something historic, something that yields as little as possible to forces and influences that are more or less new. It is on the contrary ... an expression of the age as well as an influence operating upon both present and future. (Abraham Flexner, *Universities*[1])

> Such is a University in the sphere of philosophy and research ... It is ... the high protecting power of all knowledge ... of inquiry and discovery, of experiment and speculation: it maps out the territory of the intellect and sees that ... there is neither encroachment nor surrender on either part ... It acts as an umpire between truth and truth ... it is deferential and loyal. (John Henry Newman, *The Idea of the University*[2])

Abraham Flexner's assessment, made during the great expansion of American universities (1930), speaks eloquently to the role that the institutions play with respect to the society they serve. They are an intrinsic part of the overall social fabric and exert a powerful influence on the present and the future. At the same time, they possess, as Cardinal John Henry Newman famously argued back in 1852, "the high protecting power" of intellectual inquiry and discovery that allows respite from the practical world in order ultimately to better serve it.

---

1 Abraham Flexner, *Universities, American, English, German* (London: Oxford University Press, 1930), p. 3.
2 John Henry Newmann, *The Idea of the University* (Notre Dame: University of Notre Dame Press, 1982), p. 345.

Teaching History, First Edition. William Caferro.
© 2020 John Wiley & Sons, Inc. Published 2020 by John Wiley & Sons, Inc.

It is important to add that the whole range of human emotions is played out within university walls. For students, the years are a point of passage in their lives, during which they try to figure out who they are and what they will ultimately do. For professors, the university is a proving ground for their scholarly and teacherly skill, and, indeed, a space of ongoing self-examination.

Since all colleges and universities are not created equal, the experiences are not the same. Increasingly higher standards have been set for young professors while at the same time tenure track jobs at top-tier schools have become more elusive. College administrators have more than doubled in the last 25 years, outpacing growth in the number of both students or faculty.[3] The term "corporate university" is now part of the academic lexicon. Part-time adjunct faculty account for half of instructional staffs at colleges and universities. Connecticut's Quinnipiac University employs 400 part-time faculty to supplement the 270 full-time faculty that teach its 7400 students.

But like the field of history itself, paradox and contradiction remain basic features of the academy. The marginalization of the university professor has occurred alongside the growth of teaching centers and a scholarship on pedagogy. And as studies show that the average American has less confidence that colleges and universities are preparing students well and providing good value, government and business leaders remain steadfast in their belief that universities are critically important and prefer workers who have attained higher degrees.[4]

Thus, for all the talk about "seismic shifts," "technological revolutions," "proletarianization of the workforce," and now of "culture wars 2.0," there is common ground. And, indeed, as the current scholarship on teaching and learning inclines professors toward self-reflection, this necessarily involves self-knowledge, which leads to the inevitable conclusion that there are numerous ways to achieve success even as the apparent obstacles multiply. As we collectively debate issues of teaching method and the greater role of the university in society, it is important to remember that it is how we negotiate the daily realities of the classroom and of the institutions and fields we work in that determines our effectiveness. And our ability to communicate with our students matters most of all. We fix motorcycles.

---

3 Jon Marcus, New analysis shows problematic boom in higher ed administrators. *Huffington Post* (2014). www.huffingtonpost.com/2014/02/06/higher-ed-administrators-growth_n_4738584.html

4 David J. Staley and Dennis A. Trinkle, The changing landscape of higher education. *Education Review* (January/February 2011), p. 19; Robert N. Bellah, Class and culture wars in the university today: why we cannot defend ourselves. *Academe*, 83:4 (1997), pp. 22–26.

Rich and Poor/Networks and Professionalization

To say that academia is unfair is to state a painful and obvious truth.[5] Well-to-do students are more likely to gain entrance into elite schools, just as scholars from a handful of elite graduate programs are more likely to be hired to teach them.[6] Professors at top schools have easier schedules and higher pay than those at less prestigious places. The average faculty member at Harvard University earns more than three times the wage of the average faculty member at Bethany College in West Virginia. Harvard's endowment is over 34 billion dollars while that of Fayetteville State University, an historically black institution, is only $11.4 million. There is much to James Koch's acerbic comparison of universities to types of cars: from Rolls Royces to East German Trabis.[7] Amy Kinsel, a historian at Shoreline Community College in Seattle, notes that professors in that venue also do more committee work and have salaries tied to uncertain state budgets.[8]

As noted in Chapter 2, the long view of the academy shows that elitism and stratification have always been issues. As late as the 1960s, a third of American professors did not have PhDs. And in the 1990s scholars still entered history departments that contained an old guard that had earned tenure without publication and often felt threatened by the more rigorously trained and discipline-savvy younger generation. Even as the profession grew during the "Big Bang" years, academic salaries lagged behind those of other professions, losing ground even to unskilled workers.[9] Gilbert Highet was not being ironic when he pointed to "poverty" as a basic feature of the teaching profession.[10] The cycle continues.

Given the status quo, Rebecca Schuman justifiably wondered whether going to graduate school in the humanities was worth it. In an well-written and biting essay entitled "Thesis Hatement" in *Slate* magazine (2013), Schuman concluded that it most certainly was not. "You will be broken down," she wrote, "and reconfigured in the image of the academy." When you finish, "your academic self will be the culmination of your *entire* self,

---

5 Bellah, Class and culture wars in the university today: why we cannot defend ourselves.

6 Andrew Delbanco. *College: What It Is, Was and Should Be* (Princeton: Princeton University Press, 2012).

7 James V. Koch, The multifurcation of American higher education. In: *The Future of Higher Education: Perspectives from America's Academic Leaders*, edited by Gary A. Olson and John W. Presley (Boulder: Paradigm Publishers, 2009), p. 27.

8 Amy J. Kinsel, Reflections from a community college historian. *American Historian*. https://tah.oah.org/content/reflections-from-a-community-college-historian/

9 Peter Novick, *That Noble Dream: The Objectivity Question and the American Historical Profession* (Cambridge: Cambridge University Press, 1988), p. 170.

10 Gilbert Highet, *The Art of Teaching* (New York: Vantage Books, 1950, reprint 1989), p. 10.

and thus you will believe, incomprehensibly, that not having a tenure-track job makes you worthless."[11] Schuman singles out "fat cat professors," winners of the academic sweepstakes, who hold tenured jobs at top institutions as providing a unattainable model for their students. And it is this model, as James Koch notes, that is projected to the public by major news outlets like the *New York Times*, whose myopic view of academe revolves around a few Ivy League schools, leaving the impression "that nothing is going on at 95 percent of the more than 4200 other institutions."[12] It is the experiences of a privileged few professors at the top institutions that are usually the subject of autobiographical sketches about the profession. James Banner Jr and John Gillis' *Becoming Historians* relays "the memoirs" of 11 prominent historians.[13]

Schuman's apocalyptic vision goes, however, too far and contains an all too familiar generational aspect to it. It has long been difficult to find a job: opportunities vary from field to field, and even the "fat cat" professors, upon closer examination, were often once "broken down" and "reconfigured" victims of the system. As I drifted from adjunct to assistant professor, moving about the country, unsettled financially and emotionally anxious, I took comfort in the fact that at least I was doing what I liked (reading, writing and teaching) and kept present in my mind an alternative world in which I worked an equally demanding job without the same sense of purpose and self-determination.

But Schuman's point about the identification with one's field and professional status is an important one. The system indeed ratifies its own product. The basic function of an academic discipline is to reproduce itself. And since it takes a longer time in the humanities than in other professional schools to get a PhD, the action is still more limiting and identification with the product is still greater.[14]

And it is the case that when we get our PhDs, we join a guild – a guild, in fact, of medieval origin. It has its own rules and mores, and is divided into subfields that are important in determining our professional fate. In this regard, networks lay bare the conflicting internal/external functions of the university noted by Flexner and Newman at the outset of this chapter. They necessarily reach beyond the university walls, but nevertheless exert influence on issues inside as well. We seek to publish our

11 Rebecca Schuman, "Thesis hatement," Slate (April 2013). www.slate.com/articles/life/culturebox/2013/04/there_are_no_academic_jobs_and_getting_a_ph_d_will_make_you_into_a_horrible.html
12 James V. Koch, The multifurcation of American higher education, p. 37.
13 James Banner Jr and John Gillis, *Becoming Historians* (Chicago: Chicago University Press, 2009).
14 Louis Menand, The PhD problem. *Harvard Magazine* (Nov-Dec, 2009).

work in journals in our subfields; we participate in conferences run by them and it is not hyperbole to say that our standing in the overall hierarchy of our profession depends more on them than what we do in the classroom. And as our careers progress, our participation in the networks often increases, while our interest in classroom teaching recedes.

It is important to explicitly acknowledge this aspect of the profession, because often it is ignored. Networks can enhance inequalities among professors. There are those who, for a number of reasons, are more connected and others who, for a variety of reasons, are less so. There is, in short, a rich and poor aspect here as well. But networks also provide a crucial instrument of scholarly freedom. In the face of an increasingly "corporate" administrative workforce staffed by professional bureaucrats, subfields allow scholars to establish their own standards and criteria for hires. They empower faculty, whose jobs might otherwise be reduced to a line on a budget, based on the ability to attract outside funding. Why hire several scholars in different disciplines to teach the distant past, when a school can hire a single person to teach the Middle Ages. Surely no more than one is needed?[15]

It may be for this reason that scholars often wave the banner of their subfields and identify so closely with them. There is strength in unity and the reality that rank order affects professional status. On a more existential level, belonging brings order and reassurance to an otherwise confusing professional landscape. The internet has fundamentally broadened networks, which now include "web communities" based upon a wide range of historical topics and methodologies. One can participate impersonally. A British-based website called "How to Develop Successful Networking Skills in Academia" gives detailed advice on how to deal with the different modes of interaction. It divides networking into two basic parts: "face to face" interaction, i.e., talking to people at conferences (with suggestions for conversation starters); and "electronic interaction," with suggestions on how to post questions and answer them.[16] Michael Hattem underlines the utility of social media for young scholars and graduate students. It allows them to connect with senior scholars in a "less pressurized way," by "friending" them on Facebook, commenting on a post or following them on Twitter or responding to a blog.[17]

---

15 Louis Menand, *The Marketplace of Ideas: Reform and Resistance in the American University* (New York: W.W. Norton, 2010), pp. 119, 157–158.
16 www.jobs.ac.uk/careers-advice/working-in-higher-education/573/how-to-develop-successful-networking-skills-in-academia
17 Michael D. Hattem, Academic networking 2.0: historians and social media. https://historynewsnetwork.org/article/144684

But there is undeniable inequality. Those graduate students with prominent advisors often have an advantage in access to networks over those without. And networking is more difficult for some personalities than others. Amanda Seligman of the University of Wisconsin at Milwaukee found it particularly difficult as an introverted young PhD to engage with other scholars and noted that when she became a parent, it helped her become "more socialized" both personally and professionally.[18] My own personal limitations are much the same and when I worked at my first full-time job at the University of Tulsa, there was no money for conferences, so we rarely got to go out and present work and ourselves. I was not entirely unhappy with that, although it did my career no good.

There is consolation in the research of the social network theorist Mark S. Granovetter, who has put forth the counterintuitive proposition that "weak social networks," i.e., those that do not involve close personal interaction and friendship but more casual and superficial connections, are still helpful at gaining opportunities and integration into communities.[19] More recent studies suggest, however, that "weak networks" work best when accompanied by "strong networks," with close personal ties.[20]

For the purposes here, academic networks can have both beneficial and negative effects on teaching. They introduce scholars to new trends in fields, which may then be applied to the classroom. The American Historical Association routinely holds sessions about the latest teaching methods, as do other organizations such as the National Council of History Education and the National Center for History in the Schools. The American Society of Legal Historians has recently incorporated pedagogical workshops into its national conference.[21]

But networks can also serve as competitors for a scholar/teacher's limited time. And as we become more "socialized" to them, we must take care not to confuse the language of the discourse used in that venue with that used in our classrooms. The two do not necessarily line up together. Most professors teach classes to nonspecialists and deal with social and personal issues from outside the academic world altogether.[22] Presenting conference papers for me is challenging because the mode of presentation, a formal reading coupled with an innate desire to impress my

---

18 Amanda I. Seligman, Confessions of a recovering introvert: networking when you don't want to talk to strangers. *Perspective on History* (January 5 2017).

19 Mark S. Granovetter, The strength of weak ties. *American Journal of Sociology*, 78:6 (May 1973), pp. 1360–1380.

20 Ronald S. Burt. Structural holes and good ideas. *American Journal of Sociology*, 110:2 (September 2004), pp. 349–399.

21 https://aslh.net/conference/2019-annual-meeting/

22 Louis Menand, *The Marketplace of Ideas*, pp. 157–158.

audience, runs contrary to the more accessible mode I try to summon for class. Whether this is necessarily the case for other professors is an open question, but the embedded psychologies strike me as dissimilar. I stick steadfastly to the script in the one instance and steadfastly break up the rhythm in the other. I think about myself more in the first instance and my audience more in the other.

There is, however, no more popular subject in the Vanderbilt graduate teaching seminar than networks and networking. Students see this as practical advice toward getting a job, which is the most basic goal. We work closely with members of the Vanderbilt Center for Teaching, who participate directly in the seminar as guest speakers and ongoing consultants. We include as part of the syllabus a separate section on networking and professionalization. Students have of course already contemplated such issues when they applied to graduate school. They choose programs on the strength of reputation and the likelihood that the reputation will help them get a good position. They choose research topics, guided by an advisor, with an eye on the job market. Many graduate schools now take things further and offer whole seminars on "professionalization," bringing in outsider speakers and paid consultants ("experts") to advise on interviewing technique and overall self-presentation. The professionalization seminar at the University of Southern California defines its task succinctly as teaching students how "to document and showcase skills to employers."[23]

I confess that I am among those who are not entirely comfortable with the recourse to outside "professional" experts. It threatens to put the person before the product, the cart before the horse. Professionalization is important, but the psychology can be dangerous. I have witnessed students and colleagues engage in it as an alternative to the daily stress of writing and the ego-deflating task of putting one sentence after another to make a coherent thesis argument. It is easy to deflect the one with the other. Lynn Hunt spoke eloquently on the issue when she was president of the American Historical Association. In an essay entitled "Has professionalization gone too far?" (2002), she asked whether by focusing on "professional activities," graduate students were not "buying into the illusion" that "getting a job is more important than knowing why you want one."[24] Hunt noted that supervisors often encourage students in this regard, sensitive to their needs. But she worried that students forget that professional activities take time away from writing dissertations and give

---

23 https://dornsife.usc.edu/ksi/graduate-professionalization-seminar/
24 Lynn Hunt, "Has Professionalization Gone Too Far?" *Perspectives in History* (February 2002) https://www.historians.org/publications-and-directories/perspectives-on-history/february-2002/has-professionalization-gone-too-far

the false impression that there is a "magic bullet" out there to protect them against the vicissitudes of the job market. In a similar vein, Leonard Cassuto of Fordham University has argued that the close association by students with professionalization and getting a job leads them to spend "too much time inside the lines" and thus forget that they in fact "can go outside," which Cassuto asserts is essential to intellectual creativity.[25]

Indeed, the most difficult and least discussed task is often the actual practice of writing, the process of creating, which involves the same "mundanity" and "banality" of daily practice as teaching. Graduate students are best served when they understand that by choosing to enter the professoriate, they have also chosen to make writing a fundamental part of their lives. This is what they signed on for. And inasmuch as it is not easy for most of us to get coherent thoughts out on a piece of paper (or computer screen), the process requires special vigilance. Students understand that getting into better physical shape requires a regular exercise regime of gradual increments. Medieval monks understood that piety was achieved by steps, laid out in manuals. But students do not routinely view writing this way. They see their entire existential being, their intellectual self, invested in writing assignments, which makes the process intensely difficult and entirely too personal.

In this respect, my own graduate experience, and that of my cohort, was different. It consisted of what might be best called "benign neglect," with no discussion of networking, interviewing skills or even conferences. As my colleague at Vanderbilt, Helmut Smith, who was with me in graduate school, says, "Conferences? Interviews? What are those?" when we reminisce about our mutual experience. Frank M. Turner, a historian of Victorian England at Yale University and one of the kindest and most caring professors I have ever met, told our first-year graduate class on the Scientific Revolution (by way of aside) that from this point onward we should all consider ourselves "writers and teachers," not students, and that we had to arrange our lives accordingly. Like Hunt, he advised us to develop a relationship with the study of history; if there was none, then leave and find a job more suited to your personality. Leave *without* a sense of failure. And these are words I remembered as I drifted through an itinerant professional career. The adjuncting days were actually productive ones as a scholar. And although things seemed hopeless then, the work set me up for later recognition, when I was ironically less productive.

---

25 Leonard Cassuto, "The Problem of Professionalization," *The Chronicle of Higher Education* March 23, 2015

My own views are, to be sure, colored by the limits of my own personality. I should admit that I do not like conferences or being in front of people I do not know. I avoid after-event receptions and lean heavily on the company of family and friends, who do not care or know what I do for a living. Academic networks are sometimes best served by folding one's personal life into one's professional life and thus can also serve as gossip networks about fellow scholars and personal issues, which is an aspect of the profession that I wish to avoid as much as possible.

Important recent efforts have been made in graduate schools to alter the nature of professionalization. The University of Louisville instituted a comprehensive program in 2012 for all graduate students called PLAN, organized by Beth A. Boehm and Shyam Sharm, aimed at providing professional advice that includes life skills and how to seek alternative non-professorial jobs, which is often the fate of graduate students.[26] Andrew Hoberek in "What graduate students need" suggested that graduate students would be better able to find the proper balance by receiving a course release and doing administrative work – on a labor-intensive committee or working for a journal – to get the message that "work" can mean several diverse things.[27]

The Job Search

The foregoing discussion is not intended, however, to minimize the burdens of the job search. All the discussion in the world about teaching and professionalization is irrelevant to graduate students, as Schuman forcefully argued, if there is no rainbow at the end of the yellow brick road. An important point is that nearly everyone endures humiliation and agony during the job process. Jim Boyden, a professor of early modern Spain at Tulane University, tells of opening his rejection letter from Chico State University just before he got a call for an on-campus interview at Yale University.[28] Edward Muir of Northwestern University began his distinguished career as a scholar of early modern Italy teaching at Stockton State College.

After receiving my rejection from Eastern Michigan University in Ypsilanti in 1993, a year after submitting my dissertation, I made due note of the fact that I had been rejected by every school in that state. My friend Duncan Fisher and I used to compare rejection letters. He showed

26 http://louisville.edu/graduate/plan/
27 Andrew Hoberek, What graduate students need. *Symplokē*, 10 (2002), pp. 52–70.
28 Interview with Jim Boyden.

me one that began "Dear Dr *Frisher.*" We laughed. I got one that began "Dear Dr *Camaro.*" We laughed again. In all the misspellings of my name, I had never been taken for a Chevrolet sports car. We started calling each other Dr Frisher and Dr Camaro. "How's the weather, Frisher?" "Not bad, Camaro." The irony was that the Camaro letter came from Vanderbilt University in 1994, the same place that would hire me in 1998. I thought about that letter during the 1998 job process and, of course, said nothing to anyone there. Six months or so after I arrived in Nashville, the chairman of the department, Simon Collier, a quirky and vibrant person, knocked on my door to tell me that they were shredding old documents and they had found what "appeared to be a job application" from me years earlier. I smiled and said, "Yes, and the name is Caferro not Camaro." He looked puzzled, but I did not explain.

The point is that hope rides alongside despair. It is a profession of twists and turns, and frequent failure. Although sports metaphors should be banished from civilized conversation, a comparison with baseball is not inappropriate. The most skilled batter succeeds about 30% of the time. It is how you handle failure that defines you. For this reason, I have always appreciated my job all the more. And for those colleagues who went straight from graduate school into "desirable" jobs, the road was not easier. They encountered obstacles in their surroundings, faced difficult tenure demands and institutional politics that they could not have imagined. I remember during my on-campus interviews the topic that potential future colleagues asked me most often about was my experience as an adjunct. This was often a prelude to discussion of their own difficulties. I found myself bonding with others about an experience I thought would probably be best to avoid. Indeed, when I finally got to the campus interview stage, I saw just how imperfect even ostensibly "great jobs" were up close and how everyone not only had war stories, but ultimately had to do far more than they expected to get where they are. We do well in general to avoid imagining that others do not have problems no matter what level they are in the grand hierarchy of things.

There is still no denying that the academic landscape is one of the elect and the reprobate. It is perhaps not so much strictly Calvinist, since we may, through hard work, improve our chances of redemption, if that is the right word. But factors apart from worldly calculation do play a role in our careers. And in the end, our burdens as scholars and teachers are, as noted up top, not the same, nor are our pay and status. To claim a one-to-one correspondence between hard work and status is disingenuous. Indeed, if we all set our CVs on a table for the world to see, it would not be obvious to outsiders who are the endowed professors, the full professors, associates and even adjuncts. And an examination of relative pay rates would be still more bewildering. A member of the Vanderbilt graduate teaching seminar, Aileen Teague, now a post-doc at Brown University and on the job market, notes the "profound" differences between her prior military career as a captain in the US Marines and her current experience in academia. She finds that the most basic thing to know about the history profession is that "you are your own most important advocate."[29]

Institutional/Department Culture

It is after we are hired, as new members of a department, that we engage with yet another network – not directly connected to our subfields but not entirely disconnected from them either. Each school has its own distinctive institutional culture. We navigate our institutions and departments and the specific circumstances of our hires. Wilbert McKeachie points to institutional culture in his *Teaching Tips* as a "key factor" that affects teaching strategies that faculty employ.[30]

As the circumstances differ, so too do the challenges. When I worked as an adjunct at Fairfield University, I used to go to school with a colleague, a recent PhD on the tenure track, who lived near me in New Haven. She was (and is) an excellent scholar and teacher, and a very nice person. But when we arrived at school, her face would tighten and her sense of discomfort in the department, composed exclusively of tenured middle-aged men without PhDs, was palpable, as was theirs with her. Still worse, the group treated me very warmly. I remember one afternoon, after I had been there for a few months, a faculty member called me over and asked me: "Why does she dislike us so much?" I was taken completely off guard, and responded instinctively: "I thought you didn't like *her*." The colleague looked genuinely shocked, retreated a bit, looked up at me again and said "*We* don't like *her*?" The thought had never occurred to him. I am no psychologist, but it appeared that he felt judged by her as she felt judged by him and his colleagues. There was an obvious structural problem and gender dynamic that I had missed. And as an adjunct and male, I did not figure into the dynamic at all.

The structural problems, it may be argued, reflect the white, male and elitist tradition of the historical profession (see Chapter 2). Patricia A. Matthew of Montclair State has argued in a recent essay in *The Atlantic* that faculty of color face the seemingly contradictory challenge of

---

29 Interview with Aileen Teague.
30 Wilbert McKeachie, *Tips for Teaching: A Guidebook for the Beginning College Teacher* (Lexington: D.C. Heath, 1986), p. 3.

invisibility and hypervisibility. They are often called upon to play a wide array of roles, serving on committees, mentoring and even serving as the "racial conscience" of their institutions – high-profile roles that run the risk of "ruffling feathers" and are at the same time "invisible" (i.e., not counted) with respect to earning tenure.[31] A scholar who chose to remain anonymous wrote in a piece entitled "Not just a diversity number" that he felt marginalized as a living advertisement for "diversity," which made him feel that his presence on campus turned a "little meter" in the provost's mind, with "a ker-ching" sound.[32] We have one!

Sara Ahmed in *On Being Included: Racism and Diversity in Institutional Life* makes the intriguing point that the rhetoric employed by universities about diversity may itself be part of the problem.[33] Based on interviews with "diversity officials" at universities in England and Australia, Ahmed concluded that calls for diversity ironically helped create an institutional atmosphere where racism and inequalities are overlooked. The calls were linked specifically to preexisting organizational values and university mission statements ("pursuit of academic excellence") that Ahmed argues connects diversity to what is already valued, thus maintaining rather than transforming organizational goals and with that reinforcing a species of institutional whiteness. [34]

And for all the talk by university administrations about diversity, the reality is that they have had trouble meeting their stated goals. While black students comprise about 12% of college and university enrollment, fewer than half the faculty are black. Latino professors represent only 4% of faculty nationwide, although student numbers are roughly three times higher. Data compiled by the National Center for Higher Education show that minority groups held approximately 13% of faculty jobs in 2013, up from 9% in 1993, but they held only 10% of tenured jobs. Women now comprise 49% of total faculty positions, but only 38% of tenured jobs.

And diversity is strikingly uneven; some schools like Oregon State (according to federal figures in 2016) have only 1% black faculty.[35]

31 Patricia A. Matthew, What is faculty diversity worth to a university? *The Atlantic* (November 23, 2016). www.theatlantic.com/education/archive/2016/11/what-is-faculty-diversity-worth-to-a-university/508334/, and *Written/Unwritten: Diversity and the Hidden Truths of Tenure* (Chapel Hill: University of North Carolina Press, 2016), p. 45

32 Anonymous, Not just a diversity number. *Inside Higher Education* (June 13 2012). www.insidehighered.com/advice/2012/06/13/essay-how-colleges-treat-diversity-hires

33 Sara Ahmed, *On Being Included: Racism and Diversity in Institutional Life* (Durham: Duke University Press, 2012).

34 Ahmed, *On Being Included*, p. 14.

35 Colleen Flaherty, More faculty diversity, not on tenure track. *Inside Higher Education* (August 2016). www.insidehighered.com/news/2016/08/22/study-finds-gains-faculty-diversity-not-tenure-track

The figure represents the additional factor that, as Kimberly Griffin points out, faculty of color often seek jobs in places where they feel more comfortable, in culturally diverse locations.[36]

Similar issues of invisibility and "hypervisibility" are experienced by LGBQT faculty, whose responsibilities often go far beyond the traditional academic duties at institutions that are often welcoming but whose pasts are murky. Harvard University had a committee in the 1920s to expel gay students.[37] The Florida state legislature enacted a committee in the 1950s and 1960s, the so-called Johns Committee, that harassed gay and lesbian faculty, destroying lives and careers. In addition to doing "invisible" work that does not count for promotion, faculty face the problem that their research fields are not entirely understood by colleagues, who are less able to properly assess them. And real-world politics place additional pressure on faculty, who often willingly embrace the responsibility but are not rewarded by their employers for it.

The tenure clock is particularly challenging for female faculty who wish to have children. A survey by the American Historical Association shows that women typically find their first tenured job at age 35, shortening the biological clock still further.[38] Universities have taken measures to help, but these have not always been effective or evenly applied.[39] Dana Goldberg's excellent book *The Teacher Wars*, detailing the long history of women as teachers at the primary and secondary school level, provides important perspective. She traces the "feminization of American teaching" in the nineteenth century, which brought women into the workforce, owing in large part to their perceived "domesticity" and "nurturing" quality. Women had a "peculiar power to awaken sympathies in children," and provided cheap labor, allowing men to stay in mills and undertake more "manly" pursuits.[40] Teaching was thus rendered a

---

36 Matt Krupnick, Data show the proportion of nonwhite faculty is far smaller than of nonwhite students. https://hechingerreport.org/after-colleges-promised-to-increase-it-hiring-of-black-faculty-declined/

37 Jeffrey B. Trammell, LGBT challenges in higher education today: 5 core principles for success.May/June2014.www.agb.org/trusteeship/2014/5/lgbt-challenges-higher-education-today-5-core-principles-success

38 Debbie Doyle, The tenure clock and the biological clock? *Perspectives on History* (August 26 2013). www.historians.org/publications-and-directories/perspectives-on-history/summer-2013/the-tenure-clock-and-the-biological-clock

39 Heather Antecol, Kelly Bedard and Jenna Stearns, Equal but inequitable: who benefits from gender-neutral tenure clock stopping policies? (April 2016). http://ftp.iza.org/dp9904.pdf; C. Williams and Jessica Lee, Is it time to stop stopping the clock? *Chronicle of Higher Education* (August 2016). www.chronicle.com/article/Is-It-Time-to-Stop-Stopping/237391

40 Dana Goldstein, *The Teacher Wars: A History of America's Most Embattled Profession* (New York: Anchor Books, 2014), pp. 13–32.

philanthropic vocation, a feature of primary and secondary school education that still exists today.[41]

And the legacy remains, albeit in altered form, in the university setting, where the expectation of the nurturing woman is perhaps less explicit but still palpable. Male teachers can bring their small children to class with them; women do so at the risk of becoming "mother" and thus losing a layer of teacherly authority. Female professors also find themselves placed on a disproportionate number of committees and other nontenure-related activities.

Complicating the issue further is the fact that it is not entirely clear what universities mean by diversity. The National Center for Higher Education survey in 2013 did not, for example, include as minorities non-American scholars of color and Asian-Americans. The former were left out because they "did not come from disadvantaged backgrounds" and the latter were left out because their numbers in the professoriate grew at three times the rate of the growth of white faculty.[42] The fairness of such criteria has rightly been criticized.[43] Meanwhile, faculty with disabilities contribute to diversity but they are not so easily recognized or "grouped," in large part because many, given the stigma, do not identify as such. The National Center for College Students with Disabilities reported in 2017 that 4% of university faculty admitted to disabilities, while national statistics show 22% of the general population have disabilities.[44]

Perhaps the most elusive category of all is class, which is notoriously difficult to define. In an essay entitled "Working-class lecturers should come out of the closet" in *The Guardian*, Melanie Reynolds urged "working-class" professors to identify themselves to students, who may be enduring a similar "imposter syndrome" (feeling out of place) in a higher educational system that is "dominated by the middle and upper middle class."[45] The reality, however, is that such professors often do not wish to identify themselves, or to even think about themselves in those terms,

---

41 Goldstein, *The Teacher Wars*, pp. 21, 27, 27.

42 Martin J. Finkelstein, Valerie Martin Conley and Jack H. Schuster, Taking the measure of faculty diversity. *Advancing Higher Education* (April 2016). www.tiaainstitute.org/sites/default/files/presentations/2017-02/taking_the_measure_of_faculty_diversity.pdf

43 Sharon M. Lee, Do Asian American faculty face a glass ceiling in higher education? *American Educational Research Journal*, 39:3 (Autumn 2002), pp. 695–724.

44 Joseph Grigely, The neglected demographic: faculty members with disabilities. *Chronicle of Higher Education* (June 27 2017). www.chronicle.com/article/The-Neglected-Demographic-/240439

45 Melanie Reynolds, Working-class lecturers should come out of the closet. *The Guardian* (September 2018). www.theguardian.com/commentisfree/2018/sep/10/university-working-class-divide-academics

which can be self-defeating. It may be in any case that identifying oneself to students is best done in the private of one's office hours on a person-to-person basis.[46]

The issues are still more nuanced and require far more space than is available here to discuss them fully. It is naive to assume professional solidarity based on gender, race, ethnicity, disability or class. There are categories within categories. Single women and men are sometimes asked more often to participate in committees than married faculty with children. And as universities render some faculty "hypervisible," other faculty, as a consequence, disappear. They are not asked to serve on committees or participate in university planning when in fact they may wish to do so. All human beings want to be wanted by their employers.

In the end, all politics are local, as the former Speaker of the House Tip O'Neill used to say. Preexisting personal relations in departments and circumstances of hire also affect faculty experience, as do even physical structures on campus. In my first full-time job at the University of Tulsa, the history department was small and located in a building with several other departments. Friendships developed naturally among neighbors and across disciplines and age groups. No department had critical mass or even sufficient space to create anything resembling a department "culture." The veil was in a sense lifted and we were left to our own devices. Spirited intellectual discussions took place in the halls and developed into informal reading groups. These were accompanied by informal discussions about teaching. The "socializing" process helped me prepare for class, since the discussions let me know what to expect and gave me emotional support as I stumbled forward with a new set of courses. There was little time or will to judge those who had grown cynical. It was their right, though it did not seem like an appealing way to live. I sat in my office the first day I arrived, closed the door, looked around and let the feeling of having an office sink in. I looked at the bare walls and imagined books there and thought "This is cool, really cool." I still close my door and look about my office, particularly on bad days, when teaching goes poorly and remember how fortunate I am to have one.

My career at Tulsa came to an abrupt end after my third year, when my fourth-year review – and with it my tenure track job – were suspended indefinitely, owing to financial issues at the college. It was suggested by my chairman that I look for a fellowship for the short term. I responded that I would probably have more success placing bets on horses, since

---

46 Justin Quarry, Coming out as working class. *Chronicle of Higher Education* (October 25 2018). www.chronicle.com/article/Coming-Out-as-Working-Class/244917

I had not received a fellowship previously and had been an adjunct for two years before getting my first "real" job.

Remarkably, I got a fellowship for the next year and job offers then followed – indeed, more than I could handle. I relay this story by way of offering hope to those who are experiencing difficulty, and as a cautionary tale about institutions and circumstance of hire. My professional life turned around. I went to Vanderbilt as the fortunate scholar we all hope to be coming out of graduate school. I was keenly aware, however, that nothing had in reality changed. I was the same scholar and the same teacher with the same profile. My professional value had, however, increased. I arrived in my new job discombobulated from four moves of address in two years and more than a little nervous about my new classes and surroundings.

Vanderbilt was financially solvent, had the resources to allow me to do the type of research I wanted to do and was committed to undergraduate teaching. Unlike in Tulsa, however, I encountered a definite department culture and structure. There was now a separate physical space, set off from others, and a critical mass of colleagues for a culture to flourish. There was a particularly large contingent of associate professors my age, which had made Vanderbilt still more appealing. But the circumstance proved surprisingly problematic. My professional status was higher now and the reaction to me was not the same, which I had not considered. Much of the large contingent of faculty my age, hired in close proximity immediately out of graduate school, had recently been tenured and were experiencing the infamous posttenure blues –"Is this all there is?" "Will I live forever in Nashville?" My wife and I could not really relate to this since we had already made peace with life in Tulsa, although neither of us were from that part of the world, and were thrilled to be in Nashville, which was a significant step up. And unlike elsewhere, including my jobs in secondary school, the department culture was explicitly and carefully explained to me by members of the group. It was a department of "friends," not merely colleagues. There were three "secular saints," a tradition of helping with personal issues, and two willful individuals, an assistant professor and full professor, who fell outside the good graces. The virtues of the history faculty were opposed to the lack of the same in "other departments" elsewhere and pointedly opposed to an uncaring administration.

The personal aspect was in short writ large and, indeed, the weight of numbers alone turned the professional space into a private one within my peer group. Collegiality had been crucial at Tulsa, but it was unconscious and unspoken. There were no secular saints and no outsiders. The hierarchy of virtue at Vanderbilt made me uncomfortable. I believed that it was in fact antithetical (if unintentionally) to collegiality insofar as collegiality should be measured by how well we treat those whom we find difficult and disagree with rather than how much we admire our personal friends. There seemed to me a "verticality," a collegiality piled high and deep and aimed at the top of the academic food chain, when it should have been more horizontal and evenly dispersed. I frankly had not experienced academic infighting in any of my previous jobs and, as unpopular as this is to say, I was actually grateful to the Vanderbilt administration for hiring me and for running a school that was solvent so I could move forward professionally and receive regular raises.

My priorities were in short different from my peer group, a situation that colleagues at other schools face as well. I found the history department culture intrusive. I grew instead close to the janitor, whom I saw every morning, and who had played in the Negro Leagues and would talk with me about baseball, our common love – an ongoing discussion that selfishly made me feel like myself. He brought in a bat and whiffle ball; we played together. Our baseball talk morphed into discussions of race and class, and what it was like to be a black man in the segregated South.

And when I met the "difficult" colleagues in the department, I found them as sympathetic as anyone else. There is no such thing as secular saints, nor should there be. And since my professional status had become higher when I went to Vanderbilt, I was received with greater fanfare but also with a measure of jealousy that I was completely unaccustomed to. What does one do when a secular saint acts all too human? I carried my own set experiences with me, and as I listened to the posttenure worries of others and grappled with a new and daunting set of social demands, I realized that my own professional past had effectively been erased from the public record. I was part of their discourse and that is how it would be. And when the janitor retired, I closed my office door and cried.

I then understood better the experience of my former colleague at Fairfield University, whose face would tighten whenever we arrived on campus. Groups behave differently from individuals. The circumstances of our hire, as well as social factors beyond our control, matter significantly. I was surprised by the force of my own reaction. I have met few people at the schools at which I have worked, and in academia more generally, who are not fundamentally good and kind people, despite the stereotypes about the profession. But groups often take on collective identities that are sometimes more tribal than rational. And even interpersonal relations at schools can be different depending on the degree to which they are connected to outside academic networks. There is professional capital in sainthood and a potential return on investment in friendship, if it involves befriending the right people.

In any case, whispered distinctions between "good guys" and "bad guys" among colleagues should be rejected out of hand in favor of direct personal experience. The practice is, however presented, a manifestation of an "us against them" mentality that stands at the root of so much difficulty in the world today, even if academics do not always see the parallel. We are ultimately judged by the way we treat the persons who can least help us in life.

The Appeal of Instability

The growth of teaching centers has been a conspicuously positive development in this respect, helping facilitate integration and interactions among faculty. They not only introduce faculty to new pedagogy and technology, but they bring people together across disciplines and institutional divides.[47] They alter physical space and internal departmental dynamics and act, as Sally Kuhlenschmidt of Western Kentucky University wrote, as "effective change agents" on campus.[48]

Amid the differing material and professional circumstances of professors, the basic appeal of teaching remains its inherent instability. Our professional trajectories or even personas may not be entirely in our control but when we go before a class, we enter a realm in which we bring form and meaning. Teaching is the great unknown that faculty face every semester. It is unplugged from networks, an egalitarian wild card that brings freedom, to paraphrase Marx, from the feudal ties that otherwise bind us. Success will ultimately depend on how well we prepare, how well we communicate ideas, and the jury consists of people who do not know who we are, what we have done and where we place on the greater academic scale. We do not know from year to year, day to day or even class to class what will happen. I think of it as a reality check insofar as I often get so caught up in my own world that I easily fall out of touch with the other worlds around me.

As noted throughout the book, professors cast subliminal images to students that we do not entirely control. Our race, gender, ethnicity, background, mannerisms, age, and appearance are not neutral, and do not necessarily start us off on the same footing.[49] And it is worth pointing

---

47 Susan R. Singer, Learning and teaching centers: hubs of educational reform. *New Directions for Higher Education*, 119 (2002), pp. 59–64.

48 Sally Kuhlenschmidt, Distribution and penetration of teaching-learning development units in higher education: implications for strategic planning and research. *To Improve the Academy* (June 2011), pp. 274–289; *Advancing the Culture of Teaching on Campus: How a Teaching Center Can Make a Difference*, edited by Constance Cook, Matthew Kaplan and Lester P. Monts (Sterling: Stylus Publishing 2011), p. 19.

49 Luis Ponjuan, Recruiting and retaining Latino faculty members: the missing piece to Latino student success. www.nea.org/archive/49914.htm\

out in this context that the famous school reformer Horace Mann, who was instrumental in creating the board of education in Massachusetts and wide public access to education, studied phrenology, the analysis of physical characteristics, which included the belief that Mediterraneans were "hotheads and lazy," blacks were "brutish" and northern Europeans "hard working."[50] For all his congenial advice, Gilbert Highet in *The Art of Teaching*, published in 1950, equated teaching with being a white male. He painted a pathetic portrait of the female professor, whom "girls despise ... because she is older" and "boys despise ... because she is weaker."[51] I encountered embedded gender assumptions in my Western Civilization class. I had two teaching assistants, both studying Tudor-Stuart England, both young, one male and one female. Both were hard-line graders, especially the young woman. After the first paper, a group of students, primarily women who had been in previous classes of mine, came to my office to announce "a revolt." "We have a problem with the TA." I asked which TA that was. The response was "the girl TA." I smiled and replied "as opposed then to the 'boy' TA?" Clearly, as with Highet nearly 70 years ago, the default for TA/university teacher is male. And as we talked, it became clear that there was a basic problem of authority, which was exacerbated by the youth of the TA, which in combination with gender deeply offended the students. Laura Hohman of Trivecca Nazarene College notes that as a young female professor just out of grad school, she is "frequently second guessed by students," who are more inclined to challenge the grades she gives them than those of male colleagues. She is called "ms" more often "doctor." For that reason, she prepares all the more diligently.

The dynamics of age is a subject that few teachers discuss openly. According to a medieval saying, *non est consenescendum in artibus* (from the University of Paris), "one should not grow old in the arts." This is often rendered into English as "no one likes an old student," suggesting that one should move expeditiously through one's studies. But at a more fundamental level, the aphorism opposes the arts to aging and treats growing old as a pejorative. And, indeed, for all the apparent advantages of the senior scholar, older age brings its own set of challenges with respect to teaching. Professor Susan Mosher Stuard, a retired medievalist from Haverford College, notes when she began her brilliant teaching career, she had "a more immediate relationship with students" who saw her "as part of their generation." But the relationship changed as she neared retirement, on both sides. When I first taught Western Civilization at

50 Dana Goldstein, *The Teacher Wars*, pp. 22–23.
51 Gilbert Highet, *The Art of Teaching*, p. 31.

Vanderbilt, students would come up to speak with me after the lecture. Nowadays, there is respectful distance. I answer to the term "sir," which inherently distances me from the students. In office meetings, I have learned to talk less, because if I string together more than three sentences, eyes begin to glaze over.

In this respect, we can interpret the medieval saying in a metaphorical and positive sense, as meaning that professors should always remain young in terms of their attitudes toward teaching and learning. This includes a willingness to try new things pedagogically. And whether we are young or old, our relationship with our students extends beyond the classroom. We serve as mentors. And in that role, it is, as in class, always about students first not about us. Susan Mosher Stuard, whose mentorship has guided me personally, explains that she often went out of her way "just to talk to students" outside the classroom.[52] The activity took time from scholarly work, but it was critical to the students' overall experience and paid dividends both in the classroom and outside it. I remember how Frank M. Turner, whose adopted son had been a student in my high school class, routinely invited me and other graduate students to his office to chat. That he was then provost of Yale University was a tribute to his generosity with his time. He encouraged us to ask questions that we might otherwise be reluctant to ask. I summoned my courage once and asked "How do you write a dissertation?" He smiled and said without flinching, "by steps." The first step was "to separate the process of writing from reading." Write through an idea in a concentrated, systematic way and once done, *then* print it out and start editing. The technique helps avoid getting lost in prose and editing before an idea is formed. It also helps sidestep the basic human impulse to be too perfect. "No job is so important that it cannot be done poorly the first time." The advice has stuck with me over the years, as much or more so than anything I learned in classes. Similarly, Jim Boyden, then an overburdened assistant professor at Yale, took time from his impossible schedule, during the illness of my advisors, not only to read my work but to invite me and others to his office to discuss many issues, giving us a moving image of grace under pressure.

Mentorship may be placed under the general rubric of empathy which, as noted in the first chapter, Ernest Harwell put in the still larger category of "familiarity with the human condition."[53] Extracurricular engagement is to be sure no substitute for effective classroom technique. I have never met a teacher who did not care about her/his students, but I have met some who do not convey this well. Conversely, I have met faculty who convey general personal concern well, but do not do an adequate job in the classroom.

---

52 Interview with Susan Mosher Stuard.
53 Ernest Hartwell, *The Teaching of History* (New York, 1913), p. 1.

It is a complicated relationship, and perhaps it is this aspect that inclines people to say that good teachers are born rather than developed. Human relations are intuitive. While I always felt an enormous sense of empathy for students at the front of the classroom, I found informal mentoring the hardest transition from teaching high school to teaching college. In the former, one maintains a personal distance, which was an absolute necessity. This was clear the first day that I stood behind the front desk; I was now on the other side of the law. Students consciously sought to bridge the gap, to get to know me personally. They asked me what my first name was, and other personal questions. "You can tell me, I have a brother older than you." As instructed, I kept myself vague, and reserved my humanity for the confines of classroom, for formal mentoring, and routinized behavior relating to them. There are doubtless other approaches, but as a very young-looking 23 year old, I steadfastly kept the formality. I always wore a tie to work.

I took the same attitude to college. I restricted my humanity, as it were, to the subject matter and smiled when teaching. I was in fact proud of my focus on class and on the art of teaching. The problem with the approach became apparent in my first year at Tulsa. I went in one day to my office and ran into the dean on the first floor. Two students came toward us and then stopped and stood still, watching us. The dean turned to them and asked how they were doing. They said fine and that they had stopped to say they enjoyed my class, but did not want to bother me because "he really hates it when students walk up to him after class." "He's not a 'feel-good' professor." The students smiled at that, then left. The dean, laughing, said he did not know whether to shake my hand in admiration or yell at me for being a monster. I told him I was my mother's son and that while I loved my students, I disliked the "touchy-feely" stuff and was generally awkward socially. As an adjunct at Fairfield University, I had given a surprise quiz on the day that the students evaluated my class. A colleague brought cookies. The dean at Tulsa told me that perhaps I should reconsider my attitude and understand that much good can happen outside the classroom, especially from teachers who were in fact not touchy-feely by nature. I thought about my own professors and immediately understood he was right.

Culture Wars 2.0

By way of conclusion, it is necessary to acknowledge that relations in academy have, according to many observers, become more fraught than ever. The advent of a new species of "culture war" has created a contentious environment on campus. The intensity of debate is proportional to the vastness of the medium, the internet, that propagates it. At the core of the discussion is the meaning and purpose of the university, which returns us back to the definitions of Flexner and Newman that started the chapter. The university is experiencing an identity crisis.

Contention centers on three interrelated terms: "micro-aggressions," "safe spaces," and "trigger warnings." Trigger warnings first appeared in blogs to alert victims of traumatic experiences such as sexual violence that forthcoming information might upset them or act as a "trigger." Safe spaces – described in a recent *New York Times* article as the "live-action version" of trigger warnings – are refuges for potential victims from ideas that could hurt them.[54] Micro-aggressions are small actions or word choices that may seem superficially to have no malicious intent but act as a kind of violence nonetheless.

These "polarizing concepts," as the 2016 *CNN* "guideline" to the academic year called them, have precipitated impassioned discussions.[55] Supporters see the concepts as a necessary corrective for aberrant behavior that has too long gone unchecked and as a means of inclusion of voices that have previously been marginalized and gone unheard. Opponents see the emergence of a "victimhood culture" and "empathetic correctness," by which students seek to avoid troublesome ideas. The debate has extended far beyond the campus grounds, playing out in mainstream media outlets like the *New York Times*, *The Atlantic* and the *Huffington Post* and in more specialized journals like *The Chronicle of Higher Education*. The novelist Ian McEwan has even weighed in, as has Barack Obama, in a speech in Des Moines, Iowa, in 2015, and the political/civil rights activist Van Jones. College presidents and deans have stated their views in op-ed pieces. Students have shared their feeling in blogs and social media posts. The Student Union at Columbia University started a "Micro-aggressions Project" web page that lists examples of offenses. There are similar posts at St Olaf, Oberlin and Swarthmore and other colleges.[56]

The sociologists Bradley Campbell of California State University and Jason Manning of West Virginia University (2015) see all this as reflecting a "new moral culture" in America, related to changes in social conditions.[57] Greg Lukianoff, a lawyer and CEO of the Foundation for

54 www.nytimes.com/2015/03/22/opinion/sunday/judith-shulevitz-hiding-from-scary-ideas.html
55 Emmanuela Grinberg, Trigger Warnings, safe spaces: your guide to the new school year. *CNN* (August 26 2016). www.cnn.com/2016/08/26/us/university-of-chicago-trigger-warnings-safe-spaces/index.html
56 www.microaggressions.com; http://stolafmicroaggressions-blog.tumblr.com; http://obiemicroaggressions.tumblr.com; http://swatmicroaggressions.tumblr.com
57 Bradley Campbell and Jason Manning, Micro-aggressions and changing moral cultures. *Chronicle of Higher Education* (July 2015). www.chronicle.com/article/Microaggression Changing/231395?cid=rclink

Individual Rights in Education, and Jonathan Haidt, a social psychologist, take a more critical view ("The coddling of the American mind"). They see an "undirected" student movement that seeks "to scrub campuses clean of words, ideas, and subjects that might cause discomfort or give offense."[58] They argue that universities should strongly discourage such practices, which presume "an extraordinary fragility of the collegiate psyche" and ultimately prepare students poorly for professional life. They blame overly protective parents for stifling the "free-range" lifestyle of previous generations and thus giving millennials the idea that adults must do everything to protect them. Lukianoff and Haidt also cite sharp political division in America and the penchant for the sides nowadays to demonize each other, making "comfort" a higher priority than intellectual engagement."[59] The novelist Ian McEwan resorted to parody. "A strange mood has seized the almost-educated young," he wrote in *Nutshell*, "should inconvenient opinions hover near me ... I'll be in need of the special campus safe room equipped with Play-Doh and looped footage of gamboling puppies."[60]

McEwan's statement is not just fiction. Indeed, Brown University provided a "safe space," with cookies, coloring books, Play-Doh, and a video of puppies, to soothe students whose emotions may have been 'triggered' by a university-sponsored debate between Jessica Valenti, the founder of feministing.com, and Wendy McElroy, a libertarian, about campus sexual assault. The University of California system issued a list of micro-aggressions to deans and department chairs during the 2014–15 school year, isolating six themes (including "ascription of intelligence" and "myth of meritocracy") that should be avoided by faculty.[61] Oberlin College initiated a policy in 2013 that condemned possible trigger topics such as "racism," "classism," "sexism," and "heterosexism."

The issues have often pitted administrators and faculty against each other. Oberlin's policy was rescinded "for further review" owing to faculty opposition. The American Association of University Professors' report in 2014 condemned trigger warnings on the grounds that they involve the presumption "that students need to be protected rather than challenged in a classroom, which is at once infantilizing and anti-intellectual." On the other hand, the president of Northwestern University Morton Schapiro

58 Greg Lukianoff and Jonathan Haidt, Coddling the American mind. *The Atlantic* (September 2015). www.theatlantic.com/magazine/archive/2015/09/the-coddling-of-the-american-mind/399356/
59 www.aaup.org/report/trigger-warnings
60 John Pelfry, Safe spaces are fine, but students must also be brave. *The Times Higher Education* (October 2017). www.timeshighereducation.com/opinion/safe-spaces-are-fine-students-must-also-be-brave
61 https://sites.google.com/site/cacmnow/university-of-california-microaggression-lisy

gave strong support to safe spaces after student protests about a provocative essay written by a communications professor in an opinion piece published in the *Chicago Tribune* (December 2017). He argued that safe spaces give students the courage to engage in the uncomfortable learning rather than obstruct it.[62] Across town at the University of Chicago, the dean of students sent an open letter to an incoming freshman class stating that the school did not support "trigger warnings" or "intellectual safe spaces." The letter was accompanied by a copy of *Academic Freedom and the Modern University: The Experience of the University of Chicago* by John Boyer.[63]

At base, the current debate affirms Abraham Flexner's assertion that universities are a fundamental part of the social fabric of the society they serve and map out "the territory of the intellect." On the other hand, it appears to parody Cardinal Newman's notion of "high protective power" of the university, which he envisioned as the product of rigorous intellectual exchange. In any case, the intensity of the discourse reflects, as noted above, the basic fact that college is a point of passage in the lives of young people, who are trying to figure out who they are and their place in the world. The activist Van Jones added much needed nuance, when he differentiated between good safe spaces that keep students physically safe and free of harassment on campus and bad safe spaces that offer ideological safety for those "who need to feel good all the time."[64]

Amid all the polemics, however, it is important not to overstate the novelty of current developments. Safe spaces mirror the rationale behind the establishment of women's colleges and historically black colleges during the Big Bang days. And insofar as the first all-white male American universities were tied closely to religious faith, they too represented a species of safe space. The campus as a battleground for political correctness is of course a long-standing issue. The historian Christopher Loss insightfully argues that heavy federal funding in the middle of the twentieth century turned universities into a species of "para-state" that enhanced the civic and national commitment of citizens. When the funding decreased in the 1980s, the climate at universities shifted more toward the politics of identity.[65] Current critics of safe spaces have argued along similar lines that the

---

62 www.chicagotribune.com/news/opinion/commentary/ct-perspec-safe-spaces-snowflake-myths-pc-university-universities-northwestern-university-morton-schapiro-1226-story.html
63 www.chicagotribune.com/news/local/breaking/ct-university-of-chicago-safe-spaces-letter-met-20160825-story.html
64 Flemming Rose, Safe spaces in college campuses are creating intolerant students. *Huffington Post* (June 2017). www.huffingtonpost.com/entry/safe-spaces-college-intolerant_us_58d957a6e4b02a2eaab66ccf
65 Christopher Loss, *Between Citizens and the State: The Politics of American Higher Education* (Princeton: Princeton University Press, 2011), p. 3.

recent decline in federal funding, combined with declining enrollments, has led to the "corporate" university, which treats students like consumers and caters to their personal needs rather than their education.

The notion of micro-aggressions dates in fact back to the 1970s, used then to refer primarily to racist affronts.[66] The connection between the current culture wars and prior ones is apparent in recent attempts by conservative think-tanks like the Goldwater Institute to use the "need to safeguard free speech" to try to stifle social activism on campuses, for which there is a distinguished and contentious pedigree. The Association of American University Professors has strongly condemned the Goldwater Institute as "false friends," who employ the common agenda of free speech in a "brazenly political" way to influence state legislatures, as has already occurred in North Carolina.[67] Turning Point USA, a conservative youth organization, has created a "Professor Watch List" to target "left-leaning" academics and its founder, Charlie Kirk, condemns college campuses as "islands of totalitarianism."[68]

Whether the current climate at universities reflects a new social culture, parenting skills or sharp political divides or combinations thereof, debate has traveled across the Atlantic to England, where the Prime Minister, Minister for Higher Education, and Parliament have all weighed in.[69]

The role of social media is the constant, and perhaps so self-evident that it is too easily underestimated. In this sense, technology appears to have brought about more of a revolution in the social dynamics on college campuses than in pedagogy. It has altered relationships among students, between students and faculty, and between the academy and the outside world. As noted in Chapter 3, the Web has changed the basic concept of reality and constitutes the biggest difference between the

---

66 Tazina Vega, Students see many slights as racial 'micro-aggressions.' *New York Times* (March 2014). www.nytimes.com/2014/03/22/us/as-diversity-increases-slights-get-subtler-but-still-sting.html
67 Michael C. Behrent, State of the profession: the campus free-speech movement and the AAUP (May-June 2018). www.aaup.org/article/state-profession-campus-free-speech-movement-and-aaup#.W0ksOGaZN0s
68 www.newyorker.com/news/news-desk/a-conservative-nonprofit-that-seeks-to-transform-college-campuses-faces-allegations-of-racial-bias-and-illegal-campaign-activity; Jessie Daniels and Arlene Stein, Protect scholars against attacks from the right. *Inside Higher Education* (June 26 2017). www.insidehighered.com/views/2017/06/26/why-institutions-should-shield-academics-who-are-being-attacked-conservative-groups
69 An article in April 2018 in *The Conversation* complained of transport over to England (by a graduate student in philosophy). Suzanne Whitten, Why 'safe spaces' at universities are a threat to free speech. https://theconversation.com/why-safe-spaces-at-universities-are-a-threat-to-free-speech-94547; Olivia Rudgard, Universities cannot be 'safe spaces' say MPs as they warn of 'chilling effect' on free speech. www.telegraph.co.uk/news/2018/03/27/universities-cannot-safe-spaces-say-mps-warn-chilling-effect/

current generation and previous ones. Sam Wineberg and Jose Antonio Bowen are on point when they write that the critical thinking required of history is more important than ever, And faculty themselves have been swept into the vortex. A survey in 2013 found that 55% of university faculty employ social media for professional purposes. They use it at the encouragement of book publishers to make their scholarly work more visible but some professors use the blogosphere to express their own political ideas.[70] My field of medieval history has in this way become highly politicized and the subject a heated and needlessly personal blog war in recent years.[71]

In any case, recourse to standard good/bad binaries only further erodes relations. As the foregoing discussion shows, faculty are themselves the victims of micro-aggressions, in their relations with students, with each other and the world in general. No one is free, and frustrations with the issue are exacerbated by the fact that not all transgressions fall under rubrics that can readily be quantified, or that the victims themselves would even want to be quantified. We send subliminal messages and people respond to many things, including our height, weight, tenor of voice, age, and distinguishing physical features. For instructors, who man the front lines of the culture wars, these issues come into sharp focus when we teach and expose ourselves to external scrutiny.

It is hyperbole to pronounce, as some have, the end of free speech and intellectual exchange on campuses and in classrooms. Apocalyptic visions of the future miss the mark. History, with its emphasis on the human experience, always stands at the forefront of social issues. But the current climate has not overwhelmed history classrooms. Such prognostications treat students as a monolith, when in fact they are diverse and not always as "plugged in" as presumed. And they minimize the role of professors in stimulating notions of life-long learning, which is the ultimate goal of instructors. The desire to know, as noted throughout this book, is a basic feature that connects us all across wide chasms. The rules of respectful engagement, empathy, enthusiasm, and mutual love of learning remain the guidelines. Teachers and students are allies in activism, and will continue to be. We share the experience of self-doubt, desire for affirmation and ongoing self-examination. If we perceive of the teacherly landscape as a minefield, we are more likely to step on one. Professors fix motorcycles.

---

70 Megan Rogers, Wired for teaching. *Inside Higher Education* (October 21 2013). www.insidehighered.com/news/2013/10/21/more-professors-using-social-media-teaching-tools
71 Peter Wood, Anatomy of a smear. *Inside Higher Education* (September 10 2018). www.insidehighered.com/views/2018/09/10/slurring-medieval-scholar-attempt-silence-those-who-disagree-opinion

Further Reading

Websites

- Best Teachers Institute (www.bestteachersinstitute.org)
- Carnegie Foundation for the Advancement of Teaching (www.carnegiefoundation.org)
- Center for History and New Media of George Mason University (https://chnm.gmu.edu/teaching)
- Center for Teaching, Vanderbilt University (https://cft.vanderbilt.edu)
- Goldberg Center at The Ohio State University (http://goldbergcenter.osu.edu)
- National Council of History Education (NCHE) (www.nche.net)
- National Center for History in the Schools (https://phi.history.ucla.edu/nchs)
- Centre for Historical Consciousness (www.cshc.ubc.ca)
- Roy Rosenzweig Center for Teaching and New Media (http://chnm.gmu.edu/staff/roy-rosenzweig/)
- Stanford History Education Group (https://sheg.stanford.edu)
- Zinn Educational Project (www.zinnedproject.org)

Books and Essays

Adams, Herbert Baxter. *The Study of History in American Colleges and Universities*. Washington, DC: US Government Printing Office, 1887.

Adelman, Jeremy. History a la MOOC, Version 2.0, *Perspectives on History* (2014) www.historians.org/publications-and-directories/perspectives-on-history/february-2014/historians-respond-to-moocs/history-a-la-mooc-version-20

Allitt, Patrick. *I'm the Teacher, You're the Student: A Semester in the University Classroom*. Philadelphia: University of Pennsylvania Press, 2005.

Teaching History, First Edition. William Caferro.
© 2020 John Wiley & Sons, Inc. Published 2020 by John Wiley & Sons, Inc.

Angelo, Thomas and Pat Cross. *Classroom Assessment Technique: A Handbook for College Teachers.* San Francisco: Jossey-Bass, 1993.

Altbach, Philip G. Patterns of higher education development. In: *American Higher Education in the Twenty-First Century: Social, Political and Economic Challenges,* edited by Philip G. Altbach, Patricia J. Gumport and Robert O. Berdahl. Baltimore: Johns Hopkins University Press, 2011.

Appleby, Joyce, Lynn Hunt and Margaret C. Jacob, eds. *Telling the Truth About History.* New York: W. W. Norton, 1994.

Augustine of Hippo. *Confessions.* New York: Everyman, 1907.

Bain, Ken. *What the Best College Teachers Do.* Cambridge: Harvard University Press, 2004.

Banner Jr, James and John Gillis, *Becoming Historians.* Chicago: University of Chicago Press, 2009.

Bauerlein, Mark. *The Dumbest Generation: How the Digital Age Stupefies Young Americans and Jeopardizes Our Future (Or, Don't Trust Anyone Under 30).* New York: Jeremy P. Tarcher/Penguin, 2008.

Beach, Andrea L., Mary Deane Sorcinelli, Anne E. Austin and Jacklyn K. Rivard. *Faculty Development in the Age of Evidence: Current Practices, Future Imperatives.* Sterling: Stylus Publishing, 2016.

Bean, John C. *Engaging Ideas: The Professor's Guide to Integrating Writing, Critical Thinking, and Active Learning in the Classroom.* San Francisco: Jossey-Bass, 2011.

Bender, Thomas, Colin Palmer and Philip Katz. *The Education of the Historian for the 21st Century.* Urbana: University of Illinois Press, 2004.

Bellah, Robert. Class wars and culture wars in the university today. Why we can't defend ourselves. *Academe* 83:4 (1997), pp. 22–26.

Bloch, Marc. *The Historian's Craft.* New York: Alfred A. Knopf, 1953.

Bloom, Allan. *The Closing of the American Mind.* New York: Simon & Schuster, 1987.

Bodenhamer, David J., John Corrigan, and Trevor M. Harris, eds. *The Spatial Humanities: GIS and the Future of Humanities Scholarship.* Bloomington: Indiana University Press, 2010.

Boehrer, John and Marty Linsky. Teaching with cases: learning to question. *New Directions for Teaching and Learning,* 42 (Summer 1990).

Boice, Robert. *Advice to New Faculty: Nihil Nimus.* San Francisco: Jossey-Bass, 2002.

Bok, Derek. *Universities in the Marketplace: The Commercialization of Higher Education.* Princeton: Princeton University Press, 2009.

Booth, Alan. Rethinking the scholarly: developing the scholarship of teaching in history. *Arts and Humanities in Higher Education* 3:3 (2004).

Boyer, Ernest. *Scholarship Reconsidered: Priorities of the Professoriate.* San Francisco: Jossey-Bass, 1991.

Bowen, Jose Antonio. *Teaching Naked: How Moving Technology Out of Your College Classroom Will Improve Student Learning*. San Francisco: Jossey-Bass, 2012.

Bridenbaugh, Carl. The great mutation, *American Historical Review* 68:2 (January 1963).

Brier, Stephen. Where's the Pedagogy? The Role of Teaching and Learning in the Digital Humanities at CUNY University. https://academicworks. cuny.edu/gc_pubs/201/

Brookfield, Stephen D. *Becoming a Critically Reflective Teacher*. San Francisco: Jossey-Bass, 1995.

Brookins, Julia. Survey finds fewer students enrolling in college history courses. *Perspectives on History* (September 2016). www.historians.org/ publications-and-directories/perspectives-on-history/september-2016/ survey-finds-fewer-students-enrolling-in-college-history-courses

Bynum, Caroline Walker. Where in the Text? Symposium: In the Humanities Classroom. *Common Knowledge* 23:1 (2017).

Caferro, William. Teaching Western Civilization. *Common Knowledge* 24:3 (September 2018), pp. 366–374.

Caldor, Lendol. Uncoverage: toward a signature pedagogy for the history survey. *Journal of American History* 92:4 (March 2006).

Cantu, D. Antonio and Wilson J. Warren. *Teaching History in the Digital Classroom*. Armonk, M. E. Sharpe, 2003.

Chambliss, Daniel F. Doing what works: on the mundanity of excellence in teaching. In: *The Social Worlds of Higher Education*, edited by Bernice Pescosolido and Ronald Aminzade. Thousand Oaks: Pine Forge Press, 1999.

Cohen, Daniel and Roy Rosenzweig. *Digital History*. Philadelphia: University of Pennsylvania Press, 2005.

Conderman, Greg. Ten tips in tips on course preparation. In: *Field Guide for Teaching in a New Century: Ideas from Fellow Travelers*, edited by J. H. Shin, D. Pike, D. Rome, and B. A. Pescosolido. Thousand Oaks: Pine Forge Press, 1999.

Conway, Michael. The problem with history classes. *The Atlantic* (March 2015).

Cook, Constance, Matthew Kaplan and Lester P. Monts, eds. *Advancing the Culture of Teaching on Campus: How a Teaching Center Can Make a Difference*. Sterling: Stylus Publishing, 2011.

Clement, Mary C. *First Time in the College Classroom: A Guide for Teaching Assistants*. Lanham: Rowman and Littlefield, 2010.

Crane, Richard Teller. *The Demoralization of College Life*. Chicago: H. O. Shepard, 1911.

Davidson, Cathy N. *The New Education: How to Revolutionize the University to Prepare Students for a World in Flux*. New York: Basic Books, 2017.

Davis, Barbara Gross. *Tools for Teaching*. San Francisco: Jossey-Bass, 1993.

Davis, Richard. Bhakti in the classroom: what do students hear? *Common Knowledge* 23:1 (2017).

Delbanco, Andrew. *College: What It was, Is, and Should Be*. Princeton: Princeton University Press, 2012.

Donoghue, Frank. *The Last Professors: The Corporate University and the Fate of the Humanities*. Bronx: Fordham University Press, 2008.

Doyno, Mary Harvey. Where in the text? *Common Knowledge* 23:1 (2017).

Eakin, Marshall. Teaching the Art and Craft of Teaching History. *The National Teaching and Learning Forum* (December 2015).

Eble, Kenneth. *The Aims of College Teaching*. San Francisco: Jossey-Bass, 1983.

Elton, G. R. *The Practice of History*. London: Blackwell Press, 1967.

Filene, Peter. *The Joy of Teaching: A Practical Guide for New College Instructors*. Chapel Hill: University of North Carolina Press, 2005.

Fink, L. Dee. *Creating Significant Learning Experiences: An Integrated Approach to Designing College Courses*. San Francisco: Jossey-Bass, 2013.

Flexner, Abraham. *Universities, American, English, German* (London: Oxford University Press, 1930).

Frederick, Peter. The dreaded discussion: ten ways to start in teaching and the case method. In: *Teaching and the Case Method*, edited by Louis B. Barnes, C. Roland Christensen and Abby J. Hansen. Boston: Harvard Business School Press, 1994.

Geiger, Roger L. *The History of American Higher Education: Learning and Culture from the Founding to World War II*. Princeton: Princeton University Press, 2015.

Goldstein, Dana. *The Teacher Wars: A History of America's Most Embattled Profession*. New York: Anchor Books, 2014.

Graff, Harvey J. Teaching and historical understanding: disciplining historical imagination with historical context. *Interchange* (1999).

Grafton, Anthony. History under attack. *Perspectives on History* (January 2011). www.historians.org/publications-and-directories/perspectives-on-history/january-2011/history-under-attack

Guldi, Jo and David Armitage. *The History Manifesto*. Cambridge: Cambridge University Press, 2014.

Harris, Jill S. Using GIS to teach economics education: evidence of increasing returns to scale (July 2010). https://ssrn.com/abstract=1984971

Hartwell, Ernest. *The Teaching of History*. Boston: Houghton Mifflin, 1913.

Hegel, Georg W. F. *Lectures on the Philosophy of World History*, edited by H. B. Nisbet. Cambridge: Cambridge University Press, 1975.

Higham, John. *History: Professional Scholarship in America*. Baltimore: Johns Hopkins University Press, reprint 1989.

Highet, Gilbert. *The Art of Teaching*. New York: Alfred A. Knopf, 1950.

Himmelfarb, Gertrude. *The New History and the Old*. Cambridge: Harvard University Press, 1987.

Hume, David. Of the Study of History (1741). In: *Essays, Moral, Political and Literary*, edited by Eugene F. Miller. Indianapolis: Liberty Fund, 1984.

Hunt, Lynn. *Writing History in the Global Era*. New York: W.W. Norton, 2014.

— Teaching an on-line course. *Common Knowledge* 24:3 (2018).

Jemielniak, Dariusz. Wikipedia, a professor's best friend. *Chronicle of Higher Education* (October 13, 2014). www.chronicle.com/article/wikipedia-a-professors-best/149337

Kelly, T. Mills. *Teaching History in the Digital Age*. Ann Arbor: University of Michigan, 2013.

Kerr, Cherie. *Death by Powerpoint: How to Avoid Killing your Presentation and Sucking the Life Out of the Audience*. Santa Ana: Execuprov Press, 2001.

Kerr, Clark. *Uses of the University*, 3rd edn. Cambridge: Harvard University Press, 1982.

—, Marian L. Gade and Maureen Kawaoka. *Higher Education Cannot Escape History: Issues for the Twenty-first Century*. Albany: SUNY Press, 1994.

Kinsel, Amy J. Reflections from a community college historian. *American Historian*. https://tah.oah.org/content/reflections-from-a-community-college-historian/

Koch, James V. The multifurcation of American higher education. In: *The Future of Higher Education*, edited by Gary A. Olson and John W. Presley. Boulder: University of Colorado Press, 2000.

Lang, James. *On Course: a Week-by-Week Guide to Your First Semester of College Teaching*. Cambridge: Harvard University Press, 2008.

Lévesque, Stéphane. *Thinking Historically: Educating Students for the Twenty-First Century*. Toronto: University of Toronto Press, 2008.

Lieberg, Carolyn. *Teaching Your First College Class: A Practical Guide for New Faculty and Graduate Student Instructors*. Sterling: Stylus, 2008.

Limerick, Patricia Nelson. Aloof professors and shy students. In: *On Teaching*, edited by Mary Ann Shea, vol 1. Boulder: University of Colorado Press, 1987.

Lindsay, Peter. *The Craft of University Teaching*. Toronto: University of Toronto Press, 2018.

Magnuss, Philip W. For-profit universities and the roots of adjunctification in US higher education. *Liberal Education*, 102:2 (Spring 2016).

McKay, Elspeth and John Lenarcic, eds. *Macro-Level Learning through Massive Open Online Courses (MOOCs): Strategies*. Hershey: IGI Global, 2015.

Menand, Louis. *The Marketplace of Ideas: Reform and Resistance in the American University*. New York: W.W. Norton, 2010.

Morrison, Samuel Eliot. *The Founding of Harvard*. Cambridge: Harvard University Press, 1935.

Nash, Gary B., Charlotte Crabtree and Ross E. Dunn. *History on Trial: Culture Wars and the Teaching of the Past*. New York: Vintage Books, 1994.

Newman, John Henry. *The Idea of the University*. Indiana: University of Notre Dame Press, 1982.

Novick, Peter. *That Noble Dream: The Objectivity Question and the American Historical Profession*. Cambridge: Cambridge University Press, 1988.

Oakley, Francis. *Community of Learning: The American College and the Liberal Arts Tradition*. Oxford: Oxford University Press, 1992.

Parker, Palmer. *The Courage to Teach*, 10th edn. San Francisco: Jossy-Bass, 2007.

Pirsig, Robert M. *Zen and the Art of Motorcycle Maintenance: An Inquiry into Values*. New York: Bantam, 1988.

Richlin, Laurie. *Blueprint for Learning: Constructing College Courses to Facilitate, Assess, and Document Learning*. Sterling: Stylus Publishing, 2006.

Rosenzweig, Roy. *Clio Wired: The Future of the Past in the Digital Age*. New York: Columbia University Press, 2011.

Russell, Thomas. *The No Significant Difference Phenomenon*. Raleigh: North Carolina State Press, 1999.

Schlesinger, Arthur M. The History Situation in Colleges and Universities 1919-1920, *The Historical Outlook* 11 (1920).

Schulman, L. S. Signature Pedagogies in the Professions *Daedalus* 134 (3) (2005).

Schuman, Rebecca. Thesis hatement. *Slate* (April 2013). www.slate.com/articles/life/culturebox/2013/04/there_are_no_academic_jobs_and_getting_a_ph_d_will_make_you_into_a_horrible.html

Seixas, Peter, ed. *Theorizing Historical Consciousness*. Toronto: University of Toronto Press, 2004.

— Students' understanding of historical significance. *Theory and Research in Social Education*, 22 (1994).

Shavelson, Richard J. *Measuring College Learning Responsibility: Accountability in a New Era*. Palo Alto: Stanford University Press, 2009.

Shaw, Raymond J. Assessing the intangible in our students (July 27, 2017). www.chronicle.com/article/assessing-the-intangible-in/240744

Showalter, Elaine. *Teaching Literature* (Oxford: Blackwell, 2003).

Singer, Susan R. Learning and teaching centers: hubs of educational reform. *New Directions for Higher Education*, 119 (2002).

Sorcinelli, Mary Deane. Advancing the culture of teaching on campus: how a teaching center can make a difference. *New Directions for Teaching and Learning*, 90 (Summer 2002).

Soseki, Natsume. *Grass on the Wayside*, translated by Edwin McClellan (Ann Arbor: University of Michigan Press, 1969).

Staley, David J. and Dennis A. Trinkle. The changing landscape of higher education. *Educause Review* (January/February 2011).

Stearns, Peter, Peter Seixas and Sam Wineburg. eds. *Knowing, Teaching, & Learning History. National and International Perspectives.* New York: New York University Press, 2000.

Svensson, Patrik. Envisioning the digital humanities. In: *Debates in the Digital Humanities,* edited by Matthew K. Gold. Minneapolis: University of Minnesota Press, 2012.

Svinicki, Marilla and Wilbert J. McKeachie. *McKeachie's Teaching Tips,* 13th edn. Belmont: Wadsworth, 2011.

Thomas, P. L., ed. *Becoming and Being a Teacher: Confronting Traditional Norms to Create New Democratic Realities.* New York: Peter Lang, 2012.

Thomas, William G. Interchange, the promise of digital history. *Journal of American History* (September 2008).

Thompson, Jane. *What a Teacher Learned.* Reading: Perseus Books, 1996.

Tomlinson, Carol A. This issue: differentiated instruction. *Theory Into Practice,* 44:3 (June 2010).

— *The Differentiated Classroom: Responding to the Needs of All Learners.* Alexandria: Association for Supervision & Curriculum Development, 1999.

Townsend, Robert B. *History's Babel: Scholarship, Professionalization, and the Historical Enterprise in the United States, 1880–1940.* Chicago: University of Chicago Press, 2013.

VanSledright, Bruce A. *The Challenge of Rethinking History Education: On Practices, Theories, and Policy.* Abingdon: Routledge, 2010.

— *Assessing Historical Thinking & Understanding: Innovative Designs for New Standards.* Abingdon: Routledge, 2013.

Veblen, Thorstein. *The Higher Learning in America: A Memorandum On the Conduct of Universities by Business Men.* New York: B. W. Huebsch, 1918.

Vergerio, Pier Paolo. The character and studies befitting a free-born youth. In: *Humanist Educational Treatises,* edited by Craig W. Kallendorf. Cambridge: Harvard University Press, 2002.

Veysey, Laurence. *The Emergence of the American University.* Chicago: Chicago University Press, 1965.

Warner, John. *Why They Can't Write: Killing the Five Paragraph Essay and Other Necessities.* Baltimore: Johns Hopkins University Press, 2018.

Washburn, Jennifer. *University, Inc.: The Corporate Corruption of Higher Education.* New York: Basic Books, 2006.

Weller, Toni. *History in the Digital Age.* Abingdon: Routledge Press, 2013.

Wexler, Ellen. In online courses, students learn more by doing than by watching. *Chronicle of Higher Education* (September 2016). www.chronicle.com/blogs/wiredcampus/in-online-courses-students-learn-more-by-doing-than-by-watching/57365

Wiggins, Grant P. and Jay McTighe. *Understanding by Design*. Alexandria: Association for Supervision and Curriculum Development, 1998.

Wineburg, Sam. *Historical Thinking and Other Unnatural Acts*. Philadelphia: Temple University Press, 2001.

— *Why Learn History (When It's Already on Your Phone)*. Chicago: Chicago University Press, 2018.

Wormeli, Rick. *Differentiation: From Planning to Practice, Grades 6–12*. Westerville: Stenhouse Publishers, 2007.

Wolf, Alison. *Does Education Matter? Myths about Education and Economic Growth*. London: Penguin Books, 2002.

Index

Teaching History, First Edition. William Caferro.
© 2020 John Wiley & Sons, Inc. Published 2020 by John Wiley & Sons, Inc.